Embracing Change:
The Spiritual Path to Personal Growth

Published by: Pierre Etienne

Pierre Etienne

Table of Contents

Embracing Change:

The Spiritual Path to Personal Growth

Embracing Change:

The Spiritual Path to Personal Growth

To all of humanity,

May the winds of change guide you gently toward growth and enlightenment. May you find the seeds of transformation in every challenge, and may adaptation lead you to the unfathomable depths of your spirit and the limitless potential of your path. Let change be your ally in the quest for a more harmonious and enlightened world.

With hope and love,

Pierre Etienne

"Embracing Change: The Spiritual Path to Personal Growth"**

General Disclaimer

The content in "Embracing Change: The Spiritual Path to Personal Growth" is for educational and informational purposes only. It is designed to provide general guidance and inspiration for personal development and spiritual growth. The content is not to replace professional advice, diagnosis, or treatment. Always seek the advice of a skilled expert if you have any questions regarding a medical condition, psychological issue, or other professional matter.

Health and Wellness Disclaimer

The author of this book is not a licensed healthcare provider, therapist, or counselor. The advice and strategies shown here may not be suitable for every individual, and the reader should consult with a healthcare professional to determine what is appropriate for their specific needs. Any reliance on this book's information is solely at your own risk.

Spiritual and Personal Development Disclaimer

The spiritual practices and personal development strategies covered in this book are based on the author's personal experiences and research. Individual results may vary, and the efficacy of these practices will depend on each reader's unique circumstances and personal dedication. Readers are encouraged to use their discretion and judgment while implementing the ideas offered.

Financial Disclaimer

The book may include allusions to financial principles and practices. The author is not a financial counselor, and the content should not be considered financial advice. Readers should consult a financial advisor before making any financial decisions based on the information provided in this book.

Legal Disclaimer

The author and publisher of "Embracing Change: The Spiritual Path to Personal Growth" make no claims or guarantees regarding the accuracy, applicability, suitability, or completeness of the book's content. The information is provided "as is" with no explicit or implied guarantees. The author and publisher expressly disclaim any liability for any direct, indirect, incidental, or consequential damages resulting from the use of this book.

Endorsements

Any endorsements or testimonials in this book are based on the authors' experiences and do not guarantee similar outcomes for others. The effectiveness of the concepts and practices presented in this book will vary based on individual circumstances.

Acknowledgment

By using this book, you acknowledge that you have read and understood this disclaimer and agree to its terms. If you do not agree with these terms, you should not use the book.

This disclaimer is intended to protect both the author and the reader by outlining the scope and limitations of the content provided in "Embracing Change: The Spiritual Path to Personal Growth."

— — — — — — — — — — — — — — — — —

Special Dedication:

For the Two Pillars of My Life: In Memory of My Mother, Veleine Jean Pierre, and Honor of My Beloved Wife, Magy.

To My Mother, Veleine Jean Pierre

In the loving memory of my mother, Veleine Jean Pierre, whose spirit I feel beside me daily. Your unconditional love and selflessness have been the bedrock of my life, nurturing me with a love more significant than you held for yourself. Even though you are no longer with us, your memory is permanently imprinted in my heart.

I find comfort in knowing that you watch over me, your presence a guiding light in moments of doubt and worry. In times of anxiety, I feel your gentle spirit visiting me, offering solace and strength. Your love inspires and uplifts me, a testament to our enduring bond.

To My Beloved Wife, Magy: My Partner and Guiding Light

Thank you for being my eternal source of love and guidance.

As I write this dedication, my heart overflows with gratitude for you, Magy. This book reflects my spiritual journey and would not have existed without your unwavering support and profound influence over the past 37 years.

We met during the tender years of high school, and even then, your radiant spirit and generous heart shone brightly. You chose to share your life with me, beginning a beautiful chapter that has inspired and sustained me ever since.

You have been my partner, confidante, and guiding light, standing by me through every dream pursued and challenges faced. Your strength and resilience remind me that true partnership is rooted in unconditional love and unwavering support. As a mother, you have blessed me with three exceptional children—Pierre Arthur, Melissah, and Christelle—a testament to your nurturing spirit and guiding wisdom.

Throughout the years, you have been my sounding board, offering insights with compassion and providing a safe space to explore my spirituality. Your love is a sanctuary where I find solace and strength, teaching me that true partnership is about enhancing each other's lives.

Writing this book has been transformative, deepening my understanding of spirituality and connecting me to the divine. However, none of this would have been possible without your presence. You have been my muse, inspiring me to reflect on my experiences and share them with others.

Magy, this book is as much yours as it is mine. It is a testament to the love and support you have given me and a celebration of our shared journey. Thank you for being my partner, love, and best friend. May our future be filled with love, laughter, and shared dreams.

Embracing Change:

The Spiritual Path to Personal Growth

In loving memory of Wesner Pierre,

To a man who was more than a mentor—he was a guiding light, a steadfast pillar, and a second father to me. From the tender age of eight, your nurturing spirit and unwavering support have been my compass. Through every triumph and trial, your loving, sharing, and caring presence has shaped the very essence of who I am today.

Your wisdom has been the foundation of my spiritual, emotional, and financial successes. Your encouragement has transformed my voice into a powerful speaker, and your belief in my abilities has birthed the writer in me. Because of you, I can share my journey in this book, "Embracing Change—The Spiritual Path to Personal Growth."

Thank you, Wesner, for your profound impact on my life. Your legacy continues to inspire and guide me, and your memory will forever be cherished in the words I write and the life I live.

Epigraph

"Change is the only constant in life. One' s ability to adapt to those changes will determine your success in life."

— Benjamin Franklin

Introduction

In our rapidly evolving world, adaptability and growth are more important than ever. Change is inevitable, manifesting in our personal lives, careers, relationships, and environments. Change often elicits resistance, fear, and uncertainty regardless of its constancy. "Embracing Change: The Spiritual Path to Personal Growth" aims to guide you through navigating these changes with grace, mindfulness, and a growth mindset.

Understanding the nature of change is the first step towards embracing it. Change is not only an external phenomenon but intricately intertwined with our internal experiences and perceptions. It challenges our beliefs, tests our resilience, and drives us to explore new facets of ourselves. By delving into the spiritual aspects of change, we can transform it from a source of anxiety into a powerful catalyst for personal growth.

Spiritual growth broadens our consciousness, enriches our understanding of life, and fosters a connection with our higher selves. It entails overcoming our ego, embracing our true nature, and seeking meaning and purpose in our experiences. This book delves into various aspects of spiritual growth and offers practical tools and techniques to help you on your journey.

Fear is one of the most significant obstacles to embracing change. Fear of the unknown, failure, and losing control can all hinder our ability to progress. This book addresses these fears and provides strategies to overcome them. We may open up new avenues of development and transformation by learning to confront our anxieties with bravery and awareness.

Mindfulness is essential in navigating change. By staying present and completely engaging with our experiences, we gain clarity and insight into the nature of change. This book guides you through mindfulness practices that will help you stay grounded and centered, even amidst chaos.

Accepting impermanence is another crucial aspect of embracing change. Everything in life is transient; opposing this natural flow only leads to suffering. By embracing impermanence, we learn to let go of attachments and embrace the beauty of each moment. This book explores the concept of impermanence and provides practical exercises to help you integrate what you have learned into your daily life.

Building resilience is vital for dealing with life's ups and downs. Resilience is the ability to overcome adversity and develop stronger and more capable as a result of hardships. This book offers strategies for building resilience and developing a mindset that welcomes change as an opportunity for growth.

Understanding your life's purpose brings meaning and fulfillment. Change frequently prompts us to reevaluate our goals, values, and priorities. By aligning ourselves with our true purpose, we can navigate change with clarity and fulfillment. This book will help you discover your purpose and connect your life with it.

Positive thinking and gratitude are powerful tools for embracing change. By cultivating a positive mindset and focusing on the blessings in our lives, we can shift our perspective and approach change with optimism and enthusiasm. This book offers techniques to develop positive thinking and gratitude practices.

Embracing Change:

The Spiritual Path to Personal Growth

The journey of self-discovery is integral to embracing change. We can discover more profound layers of our true selves as we navigate life's transitions. This book offers insights and exercises to help you on your path of self-discovery.

Letting go of the past is crucial to embracing change. Holding onto old patterns, regrets, and resentments can weigh us down and hinder us from moving forward. This book guides you through releasing the past and opening yourself to new possibilities.

Creating a vision for the future is another important component of embracing change. Setting clear goals and visualizing our desired outcomes can positively change our lives. This book offers tools and techniques to help you create a compelling vision for your future.

The importance of community cannot be overstated. A support system of like-minded individuals offers encouragement, inspiration, and accountability on our growth journey. This book explores the role of community and offers suggestions for building and nurturing supportive relationships.

Spiritual practices for daily living will be a recurring theme throughout the book. Incorporating spiritual practices into our daily routine helps us stay connected to our higher selves while navigating change with grace and wisdom. This book provides practical strategies for integrating spiritual practices into your life.

Finally, this book aims to integrate change into one's life. We can live more fully and authentically by embracing change as a natural and essential part of life. This book offers guidance on how to use the journey's lessons and insights in everyday life.

"Embracing Change: The Spiritual Path to Personal Growth" is a comprehensive guide to navigating life's transitions with mindfulness, resilience, and a growth mindset. Whether you are facing a significant life change or seeking to deepen your spiritual practice, this book will provide you with the tools and inspiration to embrace change and transform your life.

Chapter 1: The Nature of Change

Change is an inevitable part of life, yet it often provokes anxiety and resistance. In this chapter, we look at the nature of change, its numerous manifestations, and the profound impact it can have on our lives. Understanding the nature of change is crucial for personal and spiritual growth, enabling us to navigate life's transitions with grace and resilience.

The Different Types of Change

There are several sorts of change, each with its characteristics and challenges. These include planned, unplanned, positive, negative, and external and internal changes.

Planned and Unplanned Changes: Planned changes are those we initiate, such as starting a new job, moving to a new city, or beginning a new relationship. These changes often come with excitement and anticipation but can also bring challenges and uncertainties. Unplanned changes, on the other hand, occur abruptly and can disrupt our sense of stability and control. Examples include losing a job, experiencing a health crisis, or going through a breakup. While these changes can be more difficult to navigate, they also offer opportunities for growth and transformation.

Positive and Negative Changes: Positive changes, such as achieving a personal goal or receiving a promotion, are generally welcomed and celebrated. However, even positive changes can bring about stress and anxiety as we adjust to new circumstances. Negative changes, such as experiencing a loss or facing a setback, can be more challenging to accept. These changes often require digging deep and discovering inner strength and resilience.

External and Internal Changes: External changes occur outside of us, such as changes in our environment, relationships, or circumstances. On the other hand, internal changes occur within us, such as changes in our thoughts, beliefs, or emotions. Both forms of change are interconnected, as external changes can trigger internal shifts and vice versa.

The Role of Perception in Navigating Change

Understanding the role of our perception is an important aspect of embracing change. How we perceive change can significantly impact our ability to navigate it. If we perceive change as a threat or a loss, we are likely to resist it and experience stress and anxiety. However, if we perceive change as an opportunity for growth and new possibilities, we are more likely to embrace it with a positive attitude.

Past experiences and cultural upbringing can influence our beliefs and attitudes toward change. If we have experienced painful or traumatic changes, we may develop a fear of change and a tendency to avoid it. Similarly, if we have been taught to value stability and predictability, we may resist change and see it disrupting our sense of order.

However, change is an inevitable part of life, and resisting it only leads to sorrow. By shifting our perception and embracing change as a natural and essential part of our path, we can use it as a powerful catalyst for personal and spiritual growth. This necessitates cultivating an open, curious, and accepting mentality.

Developing Mindfulness to Navigate Change

Mindfulness is one way to shift our perception of change. Mindfulness is the practice of staying present and fully engaging with our experiences. We can grow by practicing mindfulness.

We should be conscious of our thoughts and feelings about change and monitor them without judgment. This enables us to respond to change with greater clarity and wisdom rather than reacting out of fear or resistance.

Meditation, breathing exercises, and mindful movement are some of the strategies used to practice mindfulness. Meditation quiets the mind and promotes inner peace, while breathing exercises can help calm the nervous system and reduce stress. Mindful movements, like yoga or tai chi, can help us connect with our bodies and stay grounded during times of change.

Building Resilience to Embrace Change

Another important aspect of embracing change is building resilience. Resilience is the ability to adapt and recover from adversity. It entails cultivating inner strength, flexibility, and a positive attitude towards challenges. By building resilience, we can navigate life's ups and downs with greater ease and confidence.

Developing resilience requires caring for our physical, emotional, and mental well-being. This includes maintaining a healthy lifestyle, practicing self-care, and seeking support from others. Setting realistic goals and breaking them down into manageable steps can also help us develop resilience and stay motivated during times of change.

Practical Strategies for Embracing Change

In this chapter, we will look at various practical strategies for embracing change and transforming it into an opportunity for growth. These include:

1. **Cultivating an Open Mindset**: Embrace change with curiosity and a willingness to learn. See it as an opportunity to explore new possibilities and expand your horizons.

2. **Practicing Self-Compassion**: Be kind and compassionate towards yourself as you navigate change. Acknowledge your feelings and allow yourself to experience them without judgment.

3. **Setting Realistic Goals**: Break down your goals into manageable steps and celebrate your progress. This can help you stay motivated and focused during times of change.

4. **Seeking Support**: Reach out to friends, family, or a support group for encouragement and guidance. Having a support system can provide a sense of stability and reassurance during times of change.

5. **Engaging in Mindful Practices**: Incorporate mindfulness into your daily routine to stay grounded and focused. This can help you navigate change with greater clarity and wisdom.

By embracing change with an open mind and a growth mindset, we can turn it into a powerful catalyst for personal and spiritual growth.

Affirmations

1. I embrace change as an opportunity for growth.

2. I am resilient and can adapt to any situation.

3. Change brings new opportunities into my life.

4. I trust in the process of life and its changes.

5. I am open to new possibilities and experiences.

6. I navigate change with grace and confidence.

7. I am strong and capable of overcoming challenges.

8. I release fear and embrace change with courage.

9. I find peace amid change.

10. I welcome change as a natural part of life.

11. Change helps me discover new aspects of myself.

12. I am flexible and adapt quickly to change.

13. I see change as a path to personal growth.

14. I am grateful for the opportunities change brings.

15. I trust that change leads to positive outcomes.

16. I embrace the unknown with curiosity and openness.

17. Change helps me grow stronger and wiser.

18. I accept change with a positive attitude.

19. I am at peace with the changes in my life.

20. I am prepared to handle any change that comes my way.

21. I celebrate my ability to adapt and thrive through change.

Short Meditation

Title: Embracing Change with Mindfulness

1. Find a comfortable seated position and close your eyes.

2. Take a few deep breaths, inhaling through your nose and exhaling through your mouth.

3. Bring your attention to the present moment. Notice any thoughts, feelings, or sensations without judgment.

4. Concentrate on your breath. Feel the rise and fall of your chest with each inhale and exhale.

5. As you breathe, silently repeat the affirmation: "I embrace change with grace and ease."

6. Visualize yourself navigating change with confidence and resilience. See yourself embracing new opportunities and growing stronger.

7. Take deep breaths and repeat the affirmation for a few minutes.

8. When ready, gently open your eyes and return to the present moment.

Chapter 2: Understanding Spiritual Growth

Spiritual growth develops our consciousness, enriches our understanding of life, and cultivates a connection with our higher selves. This chapter will explore the concept of spiritual growth, its importance, and the practices that support our journey.

The Concept of Spiritual Growth

Spiritual growth is not a destination but a continuous journey of self-discovery, transformation, and enlightenment. It involves expanding our awareness, deepening our understanding of the universe and our place within it, and cultivating a profound connection with our inner selves and the divine.

Spiritual growth enables us to transcend the limitations of the ego, understand the interconnectedness of all life, and align ourselves with our higher purpose. It is about evolving into the best version of us, embracing love, compassion, and wisdom, and living a life of authenticity and integrity.

Stages of Spiritual Growth

The journey of spiritual growth can be divided into several stages, each marked by unique challenges and opportunities for transformation.

1. **Awakening**: The first stage of spiritual growth involves awakening to the knowledge that there is more to life than the

material world. This stage is often triggered by a significant life event or a profound inner experience that prompts us to question our beliefs and seek deeper meaning and purpose.

2. **Exploration**: During this stage, we explore various spiritual teachings, practices, and traditions. We may seek out spiritual mentors, read books, attend workshops, and engage in meditation, prayer, and yoga practices. This stage is characterized by curiosity, openness, and a desire to learn and grow.

3. **Integration**: As our spiritual understanding grows, we integrate our spiritual insights and practices into our daily lives. This stage involves aligning our thoughts, actions, and behaviors with our spiritual values and principles. It requires self-discipline, commitment, and a willingness to let go of old patterns and habits that no longer serve us.

4. **Transformation**: During this stage, we experience significant inner transformation as we shed layers of ego and connect with our true essence. This stage is characterized by a profound sense of inner serenity, joy, and contentment. We live more authentically, guided by our inner wisdom and intuition.

5. **Mastery**: The final stage of spiritual growth involves mastering our thoughts, emotions, and actions. We become fully aligned with our higher self and live in harmony with the universe. This stage is characterized by a deep sense of unity, compassion, and love for all beings.

Obstacles to Spiritual Growth

The path of spiritual growth is not without its challenges. Along the way, we may encounter various obstacles impeding our progress. These obstacles include:

1. **Ego**: The ego is the part of us that identifies with the material world and seeks validation and approval from external sources. It has the potential to generate illusions of separation, fear, and insecurity, preventing us from recognizing our true nature.

2. **Fear**: Fear of the unknown, failure, and losing control can all impede our spiritual growth. Fear can keep us in our comfort zones and prevent us from taking steps toward transformation.

3. **Attachment**: Attachment to material possessions, relationships, and outcomes can create resistance to change and prevent us from experiencing true freedom and liberation.

4. **Negative Beliefs**: Limiting beliefs about us and the world can impede our spiritual growth. These beliefs can keep us stuck in patterns of self-doubt, unworthiness, and lack.

5. **Distractions**: The demands and distractions of daily life can divert our attention away from our spiritual practice. Creating space for regular spiritual practice and self-reflection is crucial to staying connected to our inner selves.

Practices for Supporting Spiritual Growth

Engaging in practices that nourish our mind, body, and spirit is crucial to our spiritual growth journey. These practices include:

1. **Meditation**: Meditation is a powerful practice for quieting the mind, cultivating inner peace, and connecting with our higher self. Regular meditation can help us develop greater awareness, clarity, and intuition.

2. **Mindfulness**: Mindfulness involves staying present and fully engaging with our experiences. By practicing mindfulness, we can become more aware of our thoughts, emotions, and actions and respond to life with greater wisdom and compassion.

3. **Gratitude**: Cultivating gratitude can help us shift our focus from what is lacking to what is abundant in our lives. A gratitude practice can open our hearts and foster a sense of appreciation and contentment.

4. **Self-Reflection**: Regular self-reflection allows us to gain insights into our inner world and identify areas for growth and improvement. Journaling, introspection, and seeking feedback from trusted mentors can support this practice.

5. **Service**: Engaging in acts of service and kindness can help us connect with others and instill a sense of purpose and fulfillment. Service can also help us overcome our ego and experience the joy of giving.

6. **Connecting with Nature**: Spending time in nature can help us reconnect with the natural rhythms of life and experience a sense of amazement and wonder. Nature can be an influential teacher and healer on our spiritual journey.

Affirmations

1. I am growing spiritually every day.

2. I am open to new spiritual insights.

3. I embrace my journey of self-discovery.

4. I am connected to my higher self.

5. I release fear and embrace my true nature.

6. I am grateful for the lessons of life.

7. I trust the process of spiritual growth.

8. My inner wisdom guides me.

9. I am at peace with my spiritual journey.

10. I embrace love, compassion, and wisdom.

11. I am open to spiritual transformation.

12. I align my actions with my spiritual values.

13. I am resilient and adaptable.

14. I release negative beliefs and embrace positivity.

15. I am grateful for my spiritual growth.

16. I trust my inner guidance.

17. I am compassionate towards myself and others.

18. I am open to the flow of spiritual energy.

19. I embrace change and transformation.

20. I am grateful for the support of the universe.

21. I am at peace with my spiritual path.

Short Meditation

Title: Embracing Spiritual Growth

1. Find a comfortable seated position and close your eyes.

2. Take a few deep breaths, inhaling through your nose and exhaling through your mouth.

3. Bring your awareness to your breath. Notice the natural rhythm of your breathing.

4. Visualize a bright light above your head, representing your higher self.

5. As you breathe, imagine this light descending and enveloping your entire being.

6. Silently repeat the affirmation: "I am growing spiritually every day."

7. Feel the connection to your higher self-deepening with each breath.

8. Breathe deeply and repeat the affirmation for a few minutes.

9. When ready, gently open your eyes and return to the present moment.

Chapter 3: Overcoming Fear of Change

Fear of change is one of the primary impediments to embracing it. In this chapter, we will look at the different types of fear that can arise in the face of change, such as fear of the unknown, failure, and losing control. We will discuss strategies for overcoming these fears and turning them into opportunities for growth.

Types of Fear Related to Change

Fear is a natural response to the unknown and can manifest in many ways. Understanding our specific fears can help us address them more effectively.

Fear of the Unknown: The uncertainty associated with change can be daunting. Not knowing what lies ahead can trigger anxiety and stress. This fear often stems from our desire for predictability and control.

Fear of Failure: Change often involves stepping out of our comfort zones and taking risks. The possibility of failing can be a significant deterrent, discouraging us from pursuing new opportunities and experiences.

Fear of Losing Control: Change can make us feel like we are losing control over our lives. This fear stems from our attachment to familiar routines and their comfort.

Strategies for Overcoming Fear

While fear is a natural response, it does not have to dictate our actions. Specific strategies can help us manage and overcome our fears.

1. Acknowledge Your Fear: The first step in overcoming fear is acknowledging it. Denying or suppressing fear only increases its potency. By recognizing and naming your challenges, you can begin to address them constructively.

2. Understand the Root Causes: Think about the fundamental causes of your fear. Is it the unpredictability, the possibility of failure, or the loss of control that scares you? Understanding the root causes can help you address the specific aspects that require attention.

3. Shift Your Perspective: Consider your fear as an opportunity for growth rather than a threat. Consider the possible benefits and learning experiences that change can bring. This shift in perspective can lessen anxiety and open up new possibilities.

4. Take Small Steps: Break down the change into smaller, manageable steps. Taking incremental steps can help you gain confidence and reduce the overwhelming nature of change.

5. Seek Support: Contact friends, family, or a support group. Sharing your fears and seeking guidance can offer reassurance and make you feel less alone in your journey.

6. Practice Mindfulness: Use mindfulness practices to stay present and grounded. Mindfulness can help you manage anxiety and stay calm and focused.

7. Visualize Success: Utilize visualization techniques to envision positive outcomes. Visualizing achievement can boost your confidence and motivation to embrace change.

8. Embrace Uncertainty: Recognize that uncertainty is a natural part of life. By accepting uncertainty, you can develop resilience and adaptability, allowing you to navigate change easily.

9. Develop a Growth Mindset: Foster a mindset that views challenges as opportunities for growth. A growth mindset can help you approach change with curiosity and a willingness to learn.

10. Practice Self-Compassion: Be kind and compassionate to yourself as you face your fears. Accept that it is natural to feel scared, and allow yourself to take things at your own pace.

Transforming Fear into Growth

Fear can be a powerful catalyst for growth if we learn to harness it constructively. We can discover new strengths, build resilience, and unlock our potential by confronting our fears and stepping out of our comfort zones.

1. Embrace Vulnerability: Be willing to be vulnerable and open to new experiences. Vulnerability can lead to deeper connections and more incredible personal growth.

2. Learn from Failure: Instead of viewing failure as a setback, view it as a learning opportunity. Each failure offers valuable insights and lessons to help you improve and grow.

3. Celebrate Your Progress: Acknowledge and celebrate your progress, no matter how small. Celebrating your accomplishments can boost confidence and inspire you to keep moving forward.

4. Stay Committed to Your Goals: Stay focused on your long-term goals and remind yourself of the reasons for pursuing change. Committing to your goals can provide a sense of purpose and direction.

Practical Exercises for Overcoming Fear

This chapter will look at the practical exercises to help you overcome fear and embrace change.

1. Journaling: List your fears and reflect on their remote causes. Use journaling to explore your thoughts and emotions related to change.

2. Affirmations: Use positive affirmations to reinforce your confidence and resilience. Repeat affirmations daily to shift your mindset and reduce fear.

3. Visualization: Practice visualization strategies to envisage positive outcomes. Visualize yourself effectively navigating change and achieving your goals.

4. Breathing Exercises: Deep breathing exercises can help calm your mind and reduce anxiety. Focus on your breath to stay present and focused.

5. Mindful Meditation: Practice mindful meditation to cultivate awareness and acceptance of your thoughts and emotions. Use meditation to achieve a sense of inner peace and clarity.

By effecting these strategies and exercises, you can transform fear into a powerful personal and spiritual growth force.

Affirmations

1. I am brave and embrace change with confidence.

2. I can overcome any fear that comes my way.

3. I am strong and resilient in the face of change.

4. I am open to new experiences and opportunities.

5. I am grateful for the growth from facing my fears.

6. I am in control of my responses to change.

7. I am confident in my ability to navigate uncertainty.

8. I am at peace with the unknown.

9. I am focused on the positive aspects of change.

10. I am thankful for the lessons fear teaches me.

11. I am constantly growing and evolving.

12. I am grateful for the courage within me.

13. I can embrace vulnerability with grace.

14. I am learning from every challenge and setback.

15. I am thankful for the strength fear has given me.

16. I am open to the growth that comes from change.

17. I am confident in my ability to adapt.

18. I am grateful for the support of those around me.

19. I am committed to my growth journey.

20. I am at peace with taking small steps forward.

21. I am thankful for the resilience I am building.

Short Meditation

Title: Transforming Fear into Growth

1. Find a quiet place to sit comfortably and close your eyes.

2. Take several deep breaths, inhaling through your nose and exhaling through your mouth.

3. Bring your attention to your breath, feeling the rise and fall of your chest.

4. As you breathe, imagine a soft light filling your body, bringing warmth and comfort.

5. Silently repeat the affirmation: "I am brave and embrace change confidently."

6. Visualize yourself facing and overcoming fear, feeling strong and empowered.

7. Breathe deeply and repeat the affirmation for a few minutes.

8. When ready, gently open your eyes and return to the present moment.

Chapter 4: The Role of Mindfulness

Mindfulness is a powerful tool for navigating change. In this chapter, we will look at the practice of mindfulness and how it can help us stay present and fully engaged with our experiences. We will talk about different mindfulness techniques, such as meditation, breathing exercises, and mindful movement, and how they can support us in embracing change.

The Concept of Mindfulness

Mindfulness entails being completely present in the moment and aware of our thoughts, feelings, and sensations without judgment. It is about observing our experiences with openness and curiosity rather than responding to them with habitual thinking and behavior patterns.

Mindfulness enables us to understand ourselves better and our reactions to change. It increases our awareness of our thoughts and emotions, allowing us to respond to change with greater clarity and wisdom.

Benefits of Mindfulness

Practicing mindfulness can benefit our lives, especially when navigating change. These benefits include:

1. **Increased Awareness**: Mindfulness helps us become more aware of our thoughts, emotions, and bodily sensations. This increased awareness allows us to recognize and address resistance or fear towards change.

2. **Reduced Stress**: Mindfulness practices can help alleviate stress and anxiety by encouraging relaxation and calming the mind. This can be especially helpful when dealing with the uncertainties and challenges of change.

3. **Improved Emotional Regulation**: Mindfulness promotes emotional resilience and regulation. By observing our emotions without judgment, we can respond to change with a sense of calm and composure.

4. **Enhanced Focus and Concentration**: Mindfulness helps us stay present and focused. This can enhance our decision-making and problem-solving skills, enabling us to navigate change effectively.

5. **Greater Acceptance**: Mindfulness fosters an attitude of acceptance towards our experiences. By accepting change as a natural part of life, we can let go of resistance and embrace new growth opportunities.

Mindfulness Techniques

Various mindfulness techniques can support us in embracing change. Here are some essential practices to incorporate into your daily routine:

1. Meditation: Meditation is a foundational mindfulness practice that involves focusing your attention and eliminating distracting ideas. There are several types of meditation, including focused attention, loving-kindness, and body scan.

2. Breathing Exercises: Deep breathing exercises can help calm the mind and relax the body. Diaphragmatic breathing, 4-7-8 breathing, and box breathing can reduce stress and improve mindfulness.

3. Mindful Movement: Engaging in mindful movement practices, such as yoga, tai chi, or walking meditation, can help you connect with your body and stay present. These practices combine physical movement with mindful awareness, promoting overall well-being.

4. Mindful Eating: Mindful eating entails devoting complete attention to the experience of eating, savoring each bite, and being aware of the taste, texture, and aroma of your food. This practice can improve your relationship with food and promote healthier eating habits.

5. Mindful Listening: Practice active listening by completely engaging with the person you speak to. Please observe their words, tone, and body language without interrupting or planning your response. This can improve your communication skills and strengthen your relationships.

Incorporating Mindfulness into Daily Life

To fully reap the benefits of mindfulness, it is vital to incorporate it into your daily life. Here are some tips for making mindfulness a regular part of your routine:

1. **Start Small**: Start with short mindfulness practices, such as five minutes of meditation or a few deep breaths. Gradually increase the duration and frequency of your practice as you gain more comfort.

2. **Create a Mindfulness Space**: Set aside a quiet and comfortable space in your home to practice mindfulness. This can help you establish a routine and create a sense of sacredness around your practice.

3. **Set Intentions**: Set clear goals for your mindfulness practice. Whether it is to reduce stress, improve focus, or cultivate acceptance, having a clear goal can motivate you to stay committed to your practice.

4. **Practice Throughout the Day**: Integrate mindfulness into your daily activities. Whether brushing your teeth, washing dishes, or taking a walk, practice being completely present and engaged now.

5. **Use Mindfulness Apps**: Several mindfulness apps offer guided meditations, breathing exercises, and mindfulness reminders. Apps such as Headspace, Calm, and Insight Timer can help your practice and provide additional resources.

Practical Exercises for Mindfulness

Here are some practical exercises to help you cultivate mindfulness in your daily life:

1. Mindful Breathing: Find a quiet location to sit comfortably. Close your eyes and take a few deep breaths. Focus your attention on your breath as it flows in and out. If your mind wanders, gently bring your concentration back to your breath.

2. Body Scan Meditation: Lie down in a comfortable position. Close your eyes and focus on different body parts, beginning from your toes and moving up to your head. Notice any sensations, tension, or discomfort without judgment. Take a deep breath and release any tension as you exhale.

3. Loving-Kindness Meditation: Sit comfortably and close your eyes. Take a few deep breaths and recall someone you care about. Silently repeat the phrases: "May you be happy, may you be healthy, may you be safe, may you live with ease." Extend these wishes to yourself and others.

4. Walking Meditation: Find a quiet location to stroll. Pay attention to the sensation of your feet touching the ground, the movement of your legs, and the rhythm of your breath. Stay completely present and engaged with the experience of walking.

5. Mindful Journaling: Schedule time each day to write in a journal. Reflect on your thoughts, feelings, and experiences. Write without judgment or censorship, allowing your thoughts to flow freely.

Incorporating these mindfulness practices into your daily routine enables you to develop greater awareness, reduce stress, and navigate change with greater ease and resilience.

Affirmations

1. I am present in each moment.

2. I am aware of my thoughts and feelings.

3. I am grateful for the present moment.

4. I am calm and centered.

5. I am mindful of my experiences.

6. I am open to the flow of life.

7. I am at peace with what is.

8. I am grateful for my awareness.

9. I am focused and clear-minded.

10. I am accepting my journey.

11. I am connected to the present.

12. I am grateful for the here and now.

13. I am serene and at peace.

14. I am in tune with my surroundings.

15. I am grateful for my mindfulness practice.

16. I am aware of my inner peace.

17. I am open to mindfulness.

18. I am thankful for each moment.

19. I am present with myself and others.

20. I am mindful of my breath.

21. I am grateful for my mindful heart.

Short Meditation

Title: Cultivating Mindfulness

1. Find a quiet, comfortable place to sit and close your eyes.

2. Take several deep breaths, inhaling through your nose and exhaling through your mouth.

3. Bring your attention to the natural rhythm of your breath.

4. Silently repeat the affirmation: "I am present in each moment."

5. Visualize a peaceful place, such as a serene beach or a quiet forest. Imagine yourself there, fully present and at peace.

6. As you breathe, feel the tranquility of this place filling your mind and body.

7. Breathe deeply and repeat the affirmation for a few minutes.

8. When ready, gently open your eyes and return to the present moment.

Chapter 5: Embracing Impermanence

Impermanence is an essential aspect of life, reflecting the ever-changing nature of our existence. In this chapter, we will look at the concept of impermanence and how it relates to change, personal growth, and spiritual development. By accepting impermanence, we can find peace and acceptance in the transient nature of life.

Understanding Impermanence

Impermanence, or the belief that everything is in constant flux, is a core principle in many spiritual traditions, notably Buddhism. It teaches us that everything, including our thoughts, emotions, and experiences, are temporary and subject to change.

The Relationship Between Impermanence and Change

Change is a manifestation of impermanence. Acknowledging that nothing remains the same helps us to accept and adapt to the changes we encounter. By welcoming impermanence, we can navigate life's transitions with grace and resilience, fostering personal growth and spiritual enlightenment.

Benefits of Embracing Impermanence

Embracing impermanence can bring numerous benefits to our lives, including:

1. **Increased Flexibility**: Recognizing life's constant changes helps us stay adaptable and open to new experiences.

2. **Reduced Attachment**: Understanding impermanence helps us let go of attachments and expectations, reducing suffering and disappointment.

3. **Enhanced Presence**: Being aware of the fleeting nature of each moment encourages us to live more fully in the present.

4. **Deeper Appreciation**: Realizing impermanence fosters a deeper appreciation for life's transient beauty and the people we cherish.

5. **Spiritual Growth**: Embracing impermanence promotes spiritual growth by encouraging detachment from material possessions and ego-driven desires.

Techniques for Embracing Impermanence

Here are some techniques for embracing impermanence and integrating it into your daily life:

1. Practice Mindfulness: Engage in mindfulness to stay present and fully experience each moment. Focus on your breath, bodily sensations, and surroundings to deepen your awareness of the present.

2. Reflect on Nature: Observe natural cycles, such as the changing seasons and the life cycles of plants. These phenomena illustrate the concept of impermanence.

3. Let Go of Attachments: Work on releasing attachments to material possessions, relationships, and specific outcomes. Appreciate the present moment without holding onto it.

4. Meditate on Impermanence: Engage in meditation focused on impermanence. Visualize the fleeting nature of thoughts, emotions, and experiences, and learn to accept their transitory quality.

5. Embrace Change: Approach life changes with openness. View them as opportunities for growth and transformation rather than sources of fear or resistance.

6. Gratitude Practice: Cultivate gratitude for the present moment and its experiences. Acknowledge the impermanence of these moments and treasure their uniqueness.

7. Journaling: Use journaling to reflect on your experiences with impermanence. Write about the changes you observe and how they affect you.

8. Seek Spiritual Guidance: Explore spiritual teachings that highlight impermanence. Look for guidance from mentors or communities to deepen your understanding.

Practical Exercises for Embracing Impermanence

Here are some practical exercises to help you embrace impermanence and integrate it into your daily life:

Embracing Change:

The Spiritual Path to Personal Growth

1. Daily Mindfulness Practice: Set aside time each day for mindfulness meditation. Concentrate on your breath and environment to enhance present-moment awareness.

2. Nature Observation: Spend time in nature observing life's cycles. Reflect on seasonal changes and the growth and decay of plants and natural elements.

3. Letting Go Ritual: Create a ritual to release attachments. This could involve writing down what you are attached to and symbolically letting go, perhaps by burning the paper or using another method.

4. Meditation on Impermanence: Participate in meditation that emphasizes impermanence. Visualize the transient nature of thoughts and feelings, accepting their fleeting nature.

5. Embrace Change: Face changes in your life with openness. View them as opportunities for growth rather than sources of fear.

6. Gratitude Journaling: Maintain a gratitude journal where you note the moments and experiences you appreciate. Reflect on their impermanence and the value they hold.

7. Journaling on Change: Use journaling to explore your experiences with impermanence. Write about the changes you observe and how you respond to them.

8. Spiritual Exploration: Investigate spiritual teachings that focus on impermanence. Seek insight from mentors or communities to enrich your understanding.

Affirmations

1. I am grateful for the present moment.

2. I am aware of the impermanence of life.

3. I am open to the changes life brings.

4. I am at peace with the transient nature of life.

5. I am thankful for the beauty of each moment.

6. I am adaptable and flexible.

7. I can let go of attachments.

8. I am accepting of the flow of life.

9. I am grateful for the lessons of impermanence.

10. I am at peace with change.

11. I am open to new experiences and opportunities.

12. I am thankful for the growth that comes with change.

13. I am at ease with the cycles of life.

14. I am aware of the temporary nature of all things.

15. I am grateful for the present and its experiences.

16. I am at peace with the ebb and flow of life.

17. I am open to the wisdom of impermanence.

18. I am grateful for the present and its experiences.

19. I am at peace with the ebb and flow of life.

20. I am open to the wisdom of impermanence.

21. I am grateful for each moment as it comes and goes.

Short Meditation

Title: Embracing Impermanence

1. Find a quiet place to sit comfortably and close your eyes.

2. Take several deep breaths, inhaling through your nose and exhaling through your mouth.

3. Bring your attention to the natural rhythm of your breath.

4. Silently repeat the affirmation: "I am at peace with the transient nature of life."

5. Visualize the cycles of nature, such as the changing seasons or river flow. Imagine yourself flowing with these cycles, accepting the changes they bring.

6. As you breathe, feel a sense of peace and acceptance filling your mind and body.

7. Take deep breath and repeat the affirmation for a few minutes.

8. When ready, gently open your eyes and return to the present moment.

Pierre Etienne

Chapter 6: Building Resilience

Resilience is crucial for managing life's ups and downs. This chapter will examine the concept of resilience and how it aids in adapting to change. We will explore strategies for enhancing resilience, including cultivating a positive mindset, developing inner strength, and seeking support from others.

The Concept of Resilience

Resilience is the capacity to adapt and recover from difficulties. It involves cultivating inner strength, flexibility, and a positive outlook on challenges. Resilience enables us to handle change more smoothly and confidently, transforming obstacles into opportunities for personal growth.

Benefits of Resilience

Building resilience can benefit our lives, especially when facing change. These benefits include:

1. **Increased Adaptability**: Resilience allows us to adjust more effectively to new situations and environments, making us more open to change.

2. **Enhanced Problem-Solving Skills**: It fosters a proactive mindset, empowering us to find solutions to challenges and setbacks.

3. **Improved Emotional Regulation**: Resilience helps us manage our emotions, enabling us to remain calm and composed during tough times.

4. **Greater Self-Confidence**: Building resilience increases our confidence and belief in our ability to overcome difficulties.

5. **Stronger Relationships**: It helps us establish and maintain healthy relationships by encouraging empathy, communication, and support.

Strategies for Building Resilience

Here are key strategies to enhance resilience and foster a positive attitude towards change:

1. **Cultivate a Positive Mindset**: Focus on the positive sides of change and view challenges as opportunities for growth. Use positive thinking and affirmations to strengthen your mindset.

2. **Develop Inner Strength**: Engage in practices that enhance your inner resilience, such as meditation, mindfulness, and self-reflection, creating a solid foundation of inner peace.

3. **Set Realistic Goals**: Break your goals into achievable steps and celebrate your progress. Setting realistic objectives helps maintain motivation.

4. **Seek Support**: Reach out to friends, family, or support groups for encouragement and guidance. A support system provides stability and reassurance during changes.

5. **Practice Self-Care**: Attend to your physical, emotional, and mental well-being. Participate in activities that nourish your

body and mind, such as exercise, healthy eating, and relaxation techniques.

6. **Embrace Flexibility**: Be open to new experiences and adaptable to changing circumstances, as flexibility is crucial for resilience.

7. **Learn from Setbacks**: Treat setbacks as learning experiences rather than failures. Reflect on what you learned and how you can improve.

8. **Stay Connected**: Maintain strong ties with your community and loved ones, as social support is vital for building resilience.

9. **Practice Gratitude**: Foster an attitude of gratitude by recognizing the positive aspects of your life. Gratitude can shift your perspective and enhance your well-being.

10. **Foster a Growth Mindset**: Embrace challenges as opportunities for growth, allowing you to learn and evolve continuously.

Practical Exercises for Building Resilience

Here are some practical exercises to help you cultivate resilience and develop a positive attitude toward change:

1. **Resilience Journaling**: Dedicate time each day to journal about the challenges you faced and how you overcame them. Reflect on the lessons learned and the strengths gained.

2. **Positive Affirmations**: Use positive affirmations to reinforce your belief in overcoming challenges. Repeat them daily to nurture a positive mindset.

3. **Mindfulness Meditation**: Practice mindfulness meditation to foster inner peace and resilience. Focus on your breath and observe your thoughts without judgment.

4. **Goal Setting**: Establish realistic goals and break them into manageable steps. Create an action plan and celebrate your progress along the way.

5. **Gratitude Practice**: Write down three things you are grateful for each day, reflecting on how they bring joy and fulfillment to your life.

Incorporating these exercises into your daily routine can help you build resilience and foster a positive attitude towards change.

Affirmations

1. I am resilient and can overcome any challenge.

2. I am grateful for the strength within me.

3. I am adaptable and embrace change with ease.

4. I am confident in my ability to bounce back.

5. I am thankful for the growth that comes from adversity.

6. I am strong and capable.

7. I am open to new possibilities and experiences.

8. I am grateful for my support system.

9. I am calm and composed in the face of challenges.

10. I am thankful for my inner strength.

11. I am focused on my goals and progress.

12. I am resilient and can handle whatever comes my way.

13. I am grateful for the lessons learned from setbacks.

14. I am at peace with the changes in my life.

15. I am open to learning and growth.

16. I am grateful for my positive mindset.

17. I am strong and resilient.

18. I am thankful for the support of others.

19. I am confident in my ability to adapt.

20. I am grateful for the growth opportunities.

21. I am resilient and thrive through change.

Short Meditation

Title: Building Inner Resilience

1. Find a quiet place to sit comfortably and close your eyes.

2. Take several deep breaths, inhaling through your nose and exhaling through your mouth.

3. Bring your attention to the natural rhythm of your breath.

4. Silently repeat the affirmation: "I am resilient and can overcome any challenge."

5. Visualize yourself in a situation where you overcame a challenge. Feel the strength and resilience within you.

6. As you breathe, feel a sense of inner strength and confidence filling your mind and body.

7. Breathe deeply and repeat the affirmation for a few minutes.

8. When ready, gently open your eyes and return to the present moment.

Chapter 7: Finding Purpose Through Change

Change often encourages us to rethink our goals, values, and what's important to us. In this chapter, we'll discuss how to discover purpose during times of change. We'll explore why aligning with our true purpose is important and how to navigate change with a sense of direction and fulfillment.

The Importance of Purpose

Having a sense of purpose adds meaning and direction to our lives. It drives us to pursue our goals, overcome obstacles, and contribute to something bigger than ourselves. Finding purpose amidst change can lead to fulfillment and joy.

Benefits of Finding Purpose

Identifying and aligning with our true purpose can significantly enhance our lives, especially during transitions. The benefits include:

1. **Increased Motivation**: A clear purpose boosts our motivation and inspires us to reach our goals.

2. **Greater Resilience**: Purpose gives us meaning and direction, helping us stay focused and resilient when faced with change.

3. **Enhanced Fulfillment**: Living in line with our purpose brings a sense of satisfaction and joy.

4. **Improved Decision-Making**: A strong sense of purpose guides our choices, ensuring they reflect our values and aspirations.

5. **Stronger Connections**: Purpose fosters meaningful relationships with those who share our values and goals.

Steps to Finding Purpose Through Change

Here are some steps to help you discover your purpose during change and align with your true self:

1. **Reflect on Your Values**: Think deeply about your core values and what matters most to you. Consider how these can guide your decisions during change.

2. **Identify Your Strengths**: Reflect on your strengths, talents, and passions, and think about how you can use them to make a positive impact.

3. **Set Meaningful Goals**: Establish goals that resonate with your values and purpose. Create an actionable plan and take steps toward achieving these goals.

4. **Seek Inspiration**: Look for inspiration from others who have found their purpose and are living fulfilling lives. Read books, attend workshops, and connect with mentors who can support your journey.

5. **Practice Self-Reflection**: Regularly take time to reflect on your experiences and how they align with your purpose. Think

about how each challenge and change can bring you closer to your true self.

6. **Stay Open to Change**: View change as a chance for growth and self-discovery. Be receptive to new experiences and willing to adjust your path as necessary.

7. **Connect with Others**: Build relationships with individuals who share your values and aspirations. Seek support and guidance from a community that can help keep you aligned with your purpose.

8. **Engage in Acts of Service**: Contributing to others through acts of service can instill a sense of purpose and fulfillment. Look for ways to positively impact your community.

Practical Exercises for Finding Purpose

Here are some effective exercises to help you discover your purpose during times of change and connect with your true self:

1. Values Clarification: List your core values and think about how they influence your decisions and actions. Reflect on how these values can guide you through change and help you find purpose.

2. Strengths Assessment: Identify your strengths, talents, and passions. Consider how you can use these to make a meaningful contribution.

3. Goal Setting: Establish goals that resonate with your values and purpose. Create a plan and take actionable steps toward achieving it.

4. Inspiration Journal: Keep a journal of inspiring stories, quotes, and experiences. Reflect on how these inspirations can assist you in your quest for purpose.

5. Self-Reflection: Dedicate time each week to contemplate your experiences and how they relate to your purpose. Think about how challenges and changes can bring you closer to your true self.

6. Acts of Service: Seek out opportunities to serve and make a positive difference in your community. Reflect on how these actions contribute to your sense of purpose and fulfillment.

Incorporating these exercises into your daily routine can help you find purpose through change and navigate life with clarity and fulfillment.

Affirmations

1. I am discovering my true purpose.

2. I am grateful for the journey of self-discovery.

3. I am aligned with my higher purpose.

4. I am open to new possibilities and opportunities.

5. I am thankful for the clarity and direction in my life.

6. I am confident in my ability to find purpose.

7. I am grateful for my unique strengths and talents.

8. I am living a life of meaning and fulfillment.

9. I am open to the guidance of my inner wisdom.

10. I am grateful for the support of others on my journey.

11. I am committed to my personal growth and purpose.

12. I am at peace with the changes in my life.

13. I am grateful for the growth opportunities.

14. I am open to the flow of life and its changes.

15. I am thankful for the experiences that shaped my purpose.

16. I am living in alignment with my values.

17. I am grateful for the inspiration that guides me.

18. I am confident in my path and direction.

19. I am open to the wisdom of my higher self.

20. I am grateful for the journey of finding purpose.

21. I am at peace with my life's purpose.

Short Meditation

Title: Discovering Your Purpose

1. Find a comfortable seated position and close your eyes.

2. Take several deep breaths, inhaling through your nose and exhaling through your mouth.

3. Bring your attention to the natural rhythm of your breath.

4. Silently repeat the affirmation: "I am discovering my true purpose."

5. Visualize yourself living a life of purpose and fulfillment. See yourself engaging in activities that bring you joy and meaning.

6. Feel a sense of clarity and direction filling your mind and body as you breathe.

7. Breathe deeply and repeat the affirmation for a few minutes.

8. When ready, gently open your eyes and return to the present moment.

Chapter 8: The Power of Positive Thinking

Positive thinking is a powerful tool for piloting change and enhancing overall well-being. In this chapter, we'll delve into the concept of positive thinking, its benefits, and practical strategies for cultivating an optimistic mindset. We'll also explore how positive thinking can help us embrace change and transform challenges into opportunities.

The Concept of Positive Thinking

Positive thinking involves focusing on the favorable aspects of situations and maintaining an optimistic perspective. It's about seeing the glass as half full instead of half empty and finding the silver lining in difficult circumstances. Positive thinking doesn't mean ignoring challenges; rather, it's about facing them with a constructive and hopeful attitude.

Benefits of Positive Thinking

Embracing a positive mindset offers many advantages, especially when facing change. These benefits include:

1. **Better Mental Health**: Positive thinking can alleviate stress, anxiety, and depression, promoting emotional well-being and stability.

2. **Enhanced Resilience**: A positive outlook enables us to recover more effectively from setbacks and challenges, fostering a proactive approach to problem-solving.

3. **Improved Physical Health**: Positive thinking is linked to better immune function, lower blood pressure, and a reduced risk of chronic illnesses. It can also aid in quicker recovery from health issues.

4. **Increased Motivation**: An optimistic mindset boosts our motivation and determination to reach our goals, helping us stay focused and persistent despite obstacles.

5. **Stronger Relationships**: Positive thinking enhances our relationships by encouraging empathy, compassion, and effective communication, allowing us to forge and maintain healthy connections.

Strategies for Cultivating Positive Thinking

Here are some effective strategies to nurture a positive mindset and face change with optimism:

1. **Practice Gratitude**: Regularly acknowledge the positive aspects of your life by keeping a gratitude journal. Write down three things you're thankful for each day.

2. **Reframe Negative Thoughts**: Challenge and reshape negative thoughts by seeking evidence that counters them. Use positive affirmations to replace negative self-talk.

3. **Surround Yourself with Positivity**: Seek out positive influences, such as supportive friends and uplifting media. Limit

exposure to negative news and environments that drain your energy.

4. **Focus on Solutions**: When confronted with challenges, prioritize finding solutions instead of dwelling on problems. Approach difficulties with a proactive mindset, looking for opportunities to grow.

5. **Visualize Success**: Use visualization techniques to picture positive outcomes and success. Envision yourself in achieving your goals and handling change with confidence.

6. **Practice Mindfulness**: Engage in mindfulness to stay present and aware of your thoughts and emotions. This practice can help you identify negative patterns and shift your focus to the positives at the moment.

7. **Engage in Positive Activities**: Participate in activities that bring you joy and fulfillment, such as hobbies or exercise, to enhance your mood and reinforce positivity.

8. **Set Realistic Goals**: Create achievable goals and celebrate your progress. Breaking larger goals into smaller steps can help maintain motivation.

9. **Use Positive Affirmations**: Repeat affirmations daily to strengthen your positive mindset, boosting your self-confidence and resilience.

10. **Practice Self-Compassion**: Be kind to yourself, especially during tough times. Acknowledge your efforts and recognize your strengths and accomplishments.

Practical Exercises for Positive Thinking

Here are some exercises to help you cultivate positive thinking and embrace change with optimism:

1. **Gratitude Journaling**: Maintain a gratitude journal, writing down three things you appreciate each day. Reflect on the positive elements in your life.

2. **Positive Affirmations**: Create a list of affirmations that resonate with you and repeat them daily to reinforce your goals and values.

3. **Visualization**: Utilize visualization techniques to imagine positive outcomes. Picture yourself achieving your goals and navigating changes confidently.

4. **Reframing**: When negative thoughts arise, challenge and reframe them. Find evidence that contradicts your negative beliefs and replace them with constructive thoughts.

5. **Mindfulness Meditation**: Practice mindfulness meditation to stay aware of your thoughts and emotions, cultivating a sense of calm and clarity.

By incorporating these exercises into your daily life, you can foster a positive mindset and approach change with optimism and resilience.

Affirmations

1. I am grateful for the positive aspects of my life.

2. I am confident in my ability to navigate change.

3. I am open to the opportunities that change brings.

4. I am focused on finding solutions to challenges.

5. I am grateful for my inner strength and resilience.

6. I am cheerful and optimistic about the future.

7. I am thankful for the support of my loved ones.

8. I am confident in my ability to achieve my goals.

9. I am grateful for the lessons that challenges teach me.

10. I am focused on the positive aspects of every situation.

11. I am open to new possibilities and experiences.

12. I am thankful for the growth that comes from change.

13. I am confident in my ability to adapt and thrive.

14. I am grateful for the joy and fulfillment in my life.

15. I am optimistic and proactive in my approach to challenges.

16. I am thankful for the support and encouragement I received.

17. I am confident in my ability to overcome obstacles.

18. I am grateful for the opportunities for growth and improvement.

19. I am focused on the present moment and its blessings.

20. I am open to positive energy flow in my life.

21. I am grateful for my positive mindset and outlook.

Short Meditation

Title: Cultivating Positive Thinking

1. Find a quiet, comfortable place to sit and close your eyes.

2. Take several deep breaths, inhaling through your nose and exhaling through your mouth.

3. Bring your attention to the natural rhythm of your breath.

4. Silently repeat the affirmation: "I am grateful for the positive aspects of my life."

5. Visualize yourself in a positive and uplifting situation, surrounded by supportive and encouraging people.

6. As you breathe, feel a sense of positivity and optimism filling your mind and body.

7. Breathe deeply and repeat the affirmation for a few minutes.

8. When ready, gently open your eyes and return to the present moment.

Chapter 9: Gratitude as a Tool for Change

Gratitude is a transformative practice that can shift our perspective and help us handle change with grace and positivity. In this chapter, we'll delve into the concept of gratitude, its advantages, and practical ways to foster a grateful mindset. We'll also explore how gratitude can help us embrace change and discover joy during life's transitions.

The Concept of Gratitude

Gratitude involves recognizing and valuing the positive elements in our lives, regardless of their size. It encourages us to focus on what we have instead of what we lack, finding significance in our experiences. Gratitude is a mindset that can be nurtured through deliberate practice.

Benefits of Gratitude

Embracing gratitude can greatly enhance our lives, especially when we're navigating change. Here are some key benefits:

1. **Better Mental Health**: Gratitude helps lower stress, anxiety, and depression, contributing to emotional well-being and stability.

2. **Increased Resilience**: A grateful attitude enables us to recover from setbacks and face challenges with a positive outlook and a proactive mindset.

3. **Enhanced Physical Health**: Gratitude is linked to better sleep, lower blood pressure, and improved immune function, along with faster recovery from illnesses.

4. **Stronger Relationships**: Practicing gratitude fosters empathy, compassion, and effective communication, helping us build and maintain healthy connections with others.

5. **Greater Happiness**: Gratitude is closely associated with higher levels of happiness and life satisfaction, allowing us to focus on the positives and find joy in everyday moments.

Strategies for Cultivating Gratitude

To nurture a grateful mindset and embrace change, consider these strategies:

1. **Keep a Gratitude Journal**: Each day, jot down three things you're grateful for, reflecting on the positive aspects of your life and the blessings you've received.

2. **Express Appreciation**: Take time to show appreciation to others through thank-you notes or verbal acknowledgments, recognizing those who support and uplift you.

3. **Practice Mindfulness**: Engage in mindfulness to remain present and aware of the positives in your life, appreciating the beauty of each moment.

4. **Reframe Challenges**: View challenges as chances for growth and learning. Find the silver lining in tough situations and express gratitude for the lessons they provide.

5. **Celebrate Small Wins**: Acknowledge and celebrate small achievements, expressing gratitude for your progress and efforts.

6. **Engage in Acts of Kindness**: Perform acts of kindness and generosity, which can enhance your sense of gratitude and fulfillment.

7. **Visualize Gratitude**: Use visualization to imagine positive outcomes, expressing gratitude for them. Picture yourself achieving your goals and managing change gracefully.

8. **Reflect on Past Blessings**: Think back on past experiences and the blessings they brought. Show gratitude for the positive moments and the growth they inspired.

9. **Surround Yourself with Positivity**: Seek positive influences, such as supportive friends and uplifting media, while minimizing exposure to negativity.

10. **Practice Self-Compassion**: Be kind to yourself, recognize your efforts, and express gratitude for your strengths and accomplishments.

Practical Exercises for Cultivating Gratitude

Here are some hands-on exercises to help you develop gratitude and navigate change with a grateful mindset:

1. **Gratitude Journaling**: Keep a journal where you note three things you're thankful for each day, reflecting on life's positive aspects.

2. **Thank-You Notes**: Write notes of appreciation to others, acknowledging those who support and uplift you.

3. **Mindful Appreciation**: Practice mindfulness to remain present and appreciate the positives in your life.

4. **Reframing Challenges**: Look at challenges as opportunities for growth, expressing gratitude for the lessons learned.

5. **Acts of Kindness**: Perform kind gestures for others, fostering a sense of gratitude and fulfillment in the process.

6. **Visualization**: Use visualization to imagine positive outcomes and express gratitude for them, picturing your success as you navigate change.

7. **Reflect on Past Blessings**: Consider past experiences and the positive aspects they brought, expressing gratitude for the growth they facilitated.

By integrating these exercises into your daily life, you can foster a grateful mindset and approach change with positivity and resilience.

Affirmations

1. I am grateful for the blessings in my life.

2. I am thankful for the support of my loved ones.

3. I am grateful for the lessons that challenges teach me.

4. I am open to the opportunities that change brings.

5. I am thankful for my inner strength and resilience.

6. I am grateful for the beauty of each moment.

7. I am thankful for the growth that comes from change.

8. I am open to positive energy flow in my life.

9. I am grateful for my positive mindset and outlook.

10. I am thankful for the joy and fulfillment in my life.

11. I am grateful for the support and encouragement I receive.

12. I am thankful for the opportunities for growth and improvement.

13. I am grateful for my ability to adapt and thrive.

14. I am thankful for the positive aspects of every situation.

15. I am grateful for the blessings of the present moment.

16. I am thankful for the experiences that shaped my purpose.

17. I am grateful for the lessons of the past.

18. I am thankful for my ability to find joy in everyday moments.

19. I am grateful for the people who uplift and support me.

20. I am thankful for the abundance in my life.

21. I am grateful for my journey of personal growth.

Short Meditation

Title: Cultivating Gratitude

1. Find a quiet, comfortable place to sit and close your eyes.

2. Take several deep breaths, inhaling through your nose and exhaling through your mouth.

3. Bring your attention to the natural rhythm of your breath.

4. Silently repeat the affirmation: "I am grateful for the blessings in my life."

5. Visualize yourself surrounded by the people, experiences, and moments that bring you joy and fulfillment.

6. As you breathe, feel a sense of gratitude and appreciation filling your mind and body.

7. Breathe deeply and repeat the affirmation for a few minutes.

8. When ready, gently open your eyes and return to the present moment.

Chapter 10: The Journey of Self-Discovery

Self-discovery is an ongoing journey of exploring our true selves, understanding our values, and uncovering our passions. This chapter will examine the significance of self-discovery, its benefits, and practical strategies for embarking on this path. We will also discuss how self-discovery can help us navigate change with greater clarity and purpose.

The Importance of Self-Discovery

Self-discovery entails gaining a deeper understanding of who we are, what we value, and what motivates us. It involves exploring our inner selves, recognizing our strengths and weaknesses, and embracing our authentic identities. This journey is crucial for personal growth and fulfillment.

Benefits of Self-Discovery

Engaging in self-discovery can lead to numerous advantages, especially during times of change:

1. **Enhanced Self-Awareness**: It helps us become more aware of our thoughts, emotions, and behaviors, allowing for conscious choices that align with our true selves.

2. **Boosted Self-Confidence**: Understanding our strengths and values enhances our self-confidence and belief in our abilities, helping us approach change with assurance.

3. **Greater Clarity and Purpose**: Self-discovery clarifies our life goals and purpose, enabling us to set meaningful intentions and navigate change with direction.

4. **Improved Relationships**: A deeper understanding of ourselves fosters healthier and more authentic relationships, enhancing empathy and communication.

5. **Increased Resilience**: This journey strengthens our resilience by helping us recognize and utilize our inner resources, making it easier to adapt to change.

Strategies for Embarking on the Journey of Self-Discovery

Here are some strategies to help you embark on your self-discovery journey:

1. **Reflect on Your Values**: Consider your core values and what matters most to you. Think about how these values guide your decisions and actions.

2. **Identify Your Strengths**: Take time to reflect on your strengths, talents, and passions, and consider how you can use them to contribute to something greater.

3. **Explore Your Interests**: Engage in activities and hobbies that interest you. Trying new experiences can help you uncover hidden talents and passions.

4. **Practice Mindfulness**: Stay present and aware of your thoughts and emotions through mindfulness practices, gaining deeper insights into your inner world.

5. **Seek Feedback**: Ask trusted friends, family, or mentors for feedback. Their perspectives can offer valuable insights into your strengths and areas for growth.

6. **Journaling**: Maintain a journal to reflect on your thoughts, feelings, and experiences, which can help you gain clarity and self-awareness.

7. **Set Goals**: Establish meaningful goals that align with your values and purpose. Create a plan of action and take steps toward achieving these goals.

8. **Embrace Self-Compassion**: Be kind and compassionate towards yourself, acknowledging your efforts and celebrating your strengths and accomplishments.

9. **Seek Inspiration**: Look for motivation from others who have embarked on their self-discovery journey. Read books, attend workshops, and connect with mentors who can guide you along the way.

10. **Reflect on Past Experiences**: Take time to reflect on past experiences and the lessons they taught you. Consider how these moments have shaped your identity and values.

Practical Exercises for Self-Discovery

Here are some practical exercises to help you start your journey of self-discovery:

1. **Values Clarification**: Write down your core values and reflect on how they influence your decisions and actions. Think about how these values can guide you through change and help you find purpose.

2. **Strengths Assessment**: Identify your strengths, talents, and passions. Reflect on how you can leverage these strengths to contribute to something greater than yourself.

3. **Goal Setting**: Establish meaningful goals that align with your values and purpose. Develop an action plan and take steps toward achieving these goals.

4. **Inspiration Journal**: Keep a journal filled with inspiring stories, quotes, and experiences. Reflect on how these inspirations can guide your self-discovery journey.

5. **Self-Reflection**: Set aside time each week to reflect on your experiences and how they align with your purpose. Consider how changes and challenges can bring you closer to your true self.

6. **Acts of Service**: Seek opportunities to engage in acts of service that positively impact your community. Reflect on how these experiences provide a sense of purpose and fulfillment.

By incorporating these exercises into your routine, you can embark on a fulfilling journey of self-discovery and uncover your true self.

Affirmations

1. I am on a journey of self-discovery.

2. I am grateful for the opportunity to learn about myself.

3. I am open to exploring my true self.

4. I am confident in my ability to uncover my passions.

5. I am grateful for the clarity and purpose in my life.

6. I am aware of my strengths and talents.

7. I am thankful for the lessons of self-discovery.

8. I am open to new experiences and opportunities.

9. I am grateful for my journey of personal growth.

10. I am confident in my ability to navigate change.

11. I am thankful for the support of my loved ones.

12. I know my core values and what matters most to me.

13. I am grateful for the insights and wisdom I gained.

14. I am open to the flow of self-awareness.

15. I am thankful for my positive mindset and outlook.

16. I am grateful for the beauty of each moment.

17. I am aware of my true self and authentic identity.

18. I am thankful for the journey of self-discovery.

19. I am open to opportunities for growth and improvement.

20. I am grateful for my ability to adapt and thrive.

21. I am thankful for the experiences that shape my purpose.

Short Meditation

Title: Journey of Self-Discovery

1. Find a quiet, comfortable place to sit and close your eyes.

2. Take several deep breaths, inhaling through your nose and exhaling through your mouth.

3. Bring your attention to the natural rhythm of your breath.

4. Silently repeat the affirmation: "I am on a journey of self-discovery."

5. Visualize yourself exploring your inner world, uncovering your values, strengths, and passions.

6. As you breathe, feel a sense of curiosity and openness filling your mind and body.

7. Breathe deeply and repeat the affirmation for a few minutes.

8. When ready, gently open your eyes and return to the present moment.

Chapter 11: Letting Go of the Past

Letting go of the past is essential for embracing change and moving forward. This chapter will discuss the importance of releasing old patterns, regrets, and resentments, as well as practical strategies for letting go, which can lead to personal growth and greater emotional freedom.

The Importance of Letting Go

Holding onto the past can weigh us down and prevent us from fully experiencing the present. It creates emotional baggage that hinders our ability to embrace new opportunities and relationships. Letting go involves releasing past experiences, forgiving ourselves and others, and opening ourselves to new possibilities.

Benefits of Letting Go

Letting go of the past can bring numerous benefits to our lives, particularly when navigating change. These benefits include:

1. **Emotional Freedom**: Releasing old patterns and resentments frees us from emotional burdens, allowing us to experience greater peace and happiness.

2. **Improved Relationships**: Letting go of past hurts and grievances can enhance our relationships by fostering forgiveness, understanding, and empathy.

3. **Increased Self-Esteem**: Recognizing our worth and potential through the process of letting go boosts our self-esteem and confidence.

4. **Enhanced Focus and Clarity**: Releasing the past enables us to concentrate on the present moment and make conscious choices that align with our goals and values.

5. **Greater Resilience**: Letting go strengthens our ability to adapt to change and recover from setbacks, fostering a more resilient mindset.

Strategies for Letting Go

Here are some effective strategies for letting go of the past and embracing change with a sense of freedom and possibility:

1. **Acknowledge Your Emotions**: Validate your feelings related to past experiences. Allow yourself to process these emotions without judgment, recognizing their impact on your present.

2. **Practice Forgiveness**: Forgive yourself and others for past mistakes and hurts. Understand that forgiveness is a gift you give to yourself, allowing you to release resentment and move forward.

3. **Reflect on Lessons Learned**: Consider the insights gained from past experiences. Reflecting on these lessons can illuminate how they have contributed to your growth and development.

4. **Create a Letting Go Ritual**: Design a symbolic ritual to release the past. This could involve writing down grievances and burning or discarding the paper as a tangible act of letting go.

5. **Focus on the Present**: Engage in mindfulness practices to remain present. Concentrate on your breath, sensations, and surroundings to fully experience the here and now.

6. **Set Intentions for the Future**: Define clear intentions for your future that align with your values and aspirations. Create a vision for your life that inspires and motivates you.

7. **Seek Support**: Reach out to friends, family, or support groups for encouragement and guidance. Sharing your experiences can help you process emotions and release the past.

8. **Engage in Self-Care**: Prioritize your physical, emotional, and mental well-being. Nourish your body and mind through exercise, healthy eating, and relaxation techniques.

9. **Practice Gratitude**: Cultivate an attitude of gratitude by focusing on the positive aspects of your life. Express appreciation for the lessons and growth that have come from past experiences.

10. **Embrace Change**: View change as an opportunity for growth and self-discovery. Approach new experiences with an open heart and mind, welcoming the possibilities they bring.

Practical Exercises for Letting Go

Here are some practical exercises to help you let go of the past and embrace change with a sense of freedom and possibility:

1. **Journaling**: Write about your past experiences and the emotions they evoke. Reflect on the lessons learned and how to apply them to your present and future.

2. **Forgiveness Meditation**: Engage in forgiveness meditation to release resentment and cultivate compassion. Visualize yourself forgiving others and being forgiven in return.

3. **Letting Go Ritual**: Create a ritual for letting go of the past. Write down your grievances and then symbolically release them by burning or discarding the paper, signifying your intention to let them go.

4. **Mindfulness Practice**: Practice mindfulness to stay present and fully experience the current moment. Focus on your breath, sensations, and surroundings, grounding yourself in the here and now.

5. **Vision Board**: Create a vision board that represents your goals and aspirations. Use images and words that inspire and motivate you to move forward, serving as a visual reminder of your future intentions.

By incorporating these exercises into your daily routine, you can let go of the past and embrace change with a sense of freedom and possibility.

Affirmations

1. I am letting go of the past.

2. I am grateful for the lessons of my past experiences.

3. I am open to new possibilities and opportunities.

4. I am forgiving myself and others for past mistakes.

5. I am free from emotional burdens.

6. I am focused on the present moment.

7. I am grateful for my ability to move forward.

8. I am open to the flow of life and its changes.

9. I am thankful for the growth that comes from letting go.

10. I am confident in my ability to embrace change.

11. I am at peace with my past.

12. I am open to new experiences and relationships.

13. I am grateful for the wisdom gained from past experiences.

14. I am free to create a new future.

15. I am focused on my goals and aspirations.

16. I am grateful for the support of my loved ones.

17. I am at peace with the present moment.

18. I am open to opportunities for growth and improvement.

19. I am confident in my ability to adapt and thrive.

20. I am thankful for the journey of personal growth.

21. I am free to live my life fully and authentically.

Short Meditation

Title: Letting Go of the Past

1. Find a quiet place to sit comfortably and close your eyes.

2. Take several deep breaths, inhaling through your nose and exhaling through your mouth.

3. Bring your attention to the natural rhythm of your breath.

4. Silently repeat the affirmation: "I am letting go of the past."

5. Visualize yourself releasing past experiences, regrets, and resentments. See them floating away, leaving you feeling lighter and more accessible.

6. Feel a sense of peace and freedom filling your mind and body as you breathe.

7. Breathe deeply and repeat the affirmation for a few minutes.

8. When ready, gently open your eyes and return to the present moment.

Chapter 12: Creating a Vision for the Future

Creating a vision for the future is essential in embracing change and achieving personal growth. In this chapter, we will explore the importance of setting clear intentions and visualizing desired outcomes. We will discuss practical strategies for creating a compelling vision and how it can help guide our actions and decisions.

The Importance of a Vision

A well-defined vision acts as a guiding star, helping you navigate through life's uncertainties and changes. It provides direction and clarity, allowing you to make informed choices that align with your goals and values. When you have a clear vision, you're more likely to stay motivated and focused, even when faced with obstacles.

Benefits of Creating a Vision

1. **Increased Clarity**: A vision helps clarify your goals and aspirations, making it easier to set actionable steps toward achieving them.

2. **Enhanced Motivation**: A compelling vision can inspire and motivate you to take the necessary actions to realize your dreams.

3. **Greater Focus**: With a clear vision, you're better equipped to face challenges and setbacks, as you have a strong sense of purpose driving you forward.

4. **Improved Decision-Making**: Creating a vision helps ensure that your daily actions and decisions align with your long-term goals, promoting consistency in your journey.

5. **Heightened Resilience **: A vision empowers you to take control of your life, encouraging you to take proactive steps toward your desired future.

Strategies for Creating a Vision

Here are some strategies for creating a compelling vision for the future and setting clear intentions:

1. Reflect on Your Values and Goals: Think about your core values and what you want to achieve. How do these values and goals align with your vision for the future?

2. Visualize Your Desired Outcomes: Imagine your desired future using visualization techniques. Imagine yourself achieving your goals and experiencing the emotions associated with success.

3. Set Specific and Measurable Goals: Define clear, specific, and measurable goals that align with your vision. Break these goals down into actionable steps.

4. Create a Vision Board: Create a vision board with images, words, and symbols representing your desired future. Display it where you can see it regularly to inspire and motivate you.

5. Write a Vision Statement: Write a vision statement that clearly and succinctly describes your desired future. Use positive and affirming language to describe your goals and aspirations.

6. Develop an Action Plan: Create an action plan that outlines the steps you need to follow to achieve your vision. Set timelines and milestones to track your progress.

7. Stay Flexible and Open: While having a clear vision is important, stay open to adjustments and new opportunities. Be flexible in your approach and willing to adapt as needed.

8. Seek Support and Accountability: Discuss your vision with trusted friends, family, or mentors. Seek their support and accountability to stay on track and motivated.

Practical Exercises for Creating a Vision

Here are some exercises to help you establish a clear and compelling vision for your future:

1. ****Vision Meditation****: Find a quiet space, close your eyes, and visualize your ideal future. Picture yourself achieving your goals and experiencing your best life, paying attention to the details of how you feel and what you're doing.

2. **Vision Board Creation**: Collect magazines, images, and other materials to assemble a vision board. Choose visuals that resonate with your goals and dreams, arranging them on a board for daily motivation and inspiration.

3. **Goal Setting**: Write down your goals and break them into actionable steps. Create a timeline for achieving these goals, including milestones to help track your progress.

4. **Vision Statement Writing**: Draft a vision statement that encapsulates your desired future. Use positive and affirming language to clearly describe your goals and aspirations.

5. **Journaling**: Reflect in a journal on your values, goals, and vision for the future. Write about your dreams and how you plan to achieve them. Regularly revisit your entries to monitor your growth and adjust your vision as necessary.

By integrating these exercises into your routine, you can create a powerful vision for your future and maintain your commitment to your goals.

Affirmations

1. I am creating a vision for my future.

2. I am grateful for the clarity and direction in my life.

3. I am focused on achieving my goals.

4. I am confident in my ability to achieve my vision.

5. I am grateful for the motivation and drive to succeed.

6. I am open to new opportunities and possibilities.

7. I am thankful for the support and encouragement I receive.

8. I am committed to my vision and goals.

9. I am grateful for the progress I make each day.

10. I am focused on my priorities and values.

11. I am confident in my ability to overcome challenges.

12. I am thankful for the inspiration that guides me.

13. I am open to positive energy flow in my life.

14. I am grateful for my ability to adapt and thrive.

15. I am focused on creating a fulfilling and meaningful life.

16. I am thankful for the lessons and growth that come with change.

17. I am confident in my path and direction.

18. I am grateful for my journey of personal growth.

19. I am open to opportunities for growth and improvement.

20. I am thankful for the vision and goals that guide me.

21. I am confident in creating a bright and prosperous future.

Short Meditation

Title: Creating a Vision for the Future

1. Find a quiet, comfortable place to sit and close your eyes.

2. Take several deep breaths, inhaling through your nose and exhaling through your mouth.

3. Bring your attention to the natural rhythm of your breath.

4. Silently repeat the affirmation: "I am creating a vision for my future."

5. Visualize your desired future, imagining yourself achieving your goals and experiencing the emotions associated with success.

6. As you breathe, feel a sense of clarity and motivation filling your mind and body.

7. Breathe deeply and repeat the affirmation for a few minutes.

8. When ready, gently open your eyes and return to the present moment.

Chapter 13: The Significance of Community

Community is vital for our personal development and well-being. This chapter focuses on the importance of cultivating and maintaining supportive relationships. We will examine how community can assist us in navigating change, foster a sense of belonging, and enhance our purpose and fulfillment.

The Role of Community

A strong community offers emotional support, encouragement, and a sense of belonging. It connects us with individuals who share similar values and goals. Being part of a community helps us feel understood, valued, and supported, which is essential for our overall health.

Benefits of Community

Being involved in a supportive community provides numerous advantages, especially during times of change. These benefits include:

1. **Emotional Support**: The community offers a network of individuals who provide empathy, understanding, and encouragement during difficult times.

2. **Sense of Belonging**: Being part of a community creates a feeling of connection and belonging, helping to alleviate feelings of isolation and loneliness.

3. **Shared Resources and Knowledge**: Community members can exchange resources, knowledge, and experiences, offering valuable insights and guidance.

4. **Accountability and Motivation**: Community fosters accountability and motivation, aiding us in staying committed to our goals and aspirations.

5. **Enhanced Resilience**: A supportive community enhances our resilience, allowing us to adapt to change and recover from setbacks.

Strategies for Building and Nurturing Community

Here are some strategies for cultivating and nurturing a supportive community:

1. **Identify Your Values and Interests**: Reflect on your interests and goals, and seek out communities that align with these aspects of your life.

2. **Join Groups and Organizations**: Participate in groups, clubs, or organizations that resonate with your values and interests. Engage in activities and events to connect with like-minded individuals.

3. **Volunteer and Give Back**: Participate in volunteer activities to give back to your community. Volunteering fosters a sense of purpose and connection with others.

4. **Build Strong Relationships**: Dedicate time and effort to nurturing strong relationships with friends, family, and colleagues. Communicate openly, show empathy, and provide support.

5. **Attend Workshops and Events**: Join workshops, seminars, and events related to your interests and goals. These gatherings create opportunities to meet new people and expand your network.

6. **Seek Mentorship and Guidance**: Find mentors and guides who can provide support, wisdom, and encouragement on your journey.

7. **Create a Support System**: Establish a network of trusted friends, family, and mentors who can offer emotional support and encouragement.

8. **Practice Active Listening**: Engage in active listening and show genuine interest in others' experiences and perspectives. Strong relationships require mutual understanding and respect.

9. **Stay Connected**: Maintain regular communication with your community through meetings, gatherings, and social interactions. Nurture your relationships over time.

10. **Foster Inclusivity**: Create an inclusive and welcoming environment within your community. Embrace diversity and promote open, respectful dialogue.

Practical Exercises for Building Community

Here are some practical activities to help you cultivate and strengthen a supportive community:

1. Community Mapping: Draw a map of your current community, including friends, family, colleagues, and groups you belong to. Identify areas where you can enhance or broaden your connections.

2. Volunteering: Look for volunteer opportunities in your community that resonate with your interests and values. Get involved in volunteer activities and reflect on the relationships you develop.

3. Active Listening Practice: Focus on practicing active listening during conversations. Aim to understand the other person's viewpoint while demonstrating empathy and support.

4. Attend Social Events: Participate in social gatherings, workshops, and events that relate to your interests. Make an effort to meet new individuals and expand your network.

5. Support System Check-In: Regularly check in with your support network. Offer and seek help, share experiences, and stay engaged.

By integrating these exercises into your daily life, you can foster a supportive community that contributes to your personal growth and well-being.

Affirmations

1. I am grateful for my supportive community.

2. I am thankful for the connections I have with others.

3. I am open to building new relationships.

4. I am grateful for the support and encouragement I receive.

5. I am thankful for the sense of belonging in my community.

6. I am open to sharing my experiences and knowledge with others.

7. I am grateful for the empathy and understanding of my community.

8. I am thankful for the motivation and accountability my community provides.

9. I am open to giving and receiving support.

10. I am grateful for the opportunities to connect with like-minded individuals.

11. I am thankful for the resilience I gained from my community.

12. I am open to fostering inclusivity and diversity in my community.

13. I am grateful for the wisdom and guidance of my mentors.

14. I am thankful for my community's shared resources and knowledge.

15. I am open to new opportunities for connection and growth.

16. I am grateful for the strong relationships I have built.

17. I am thankful for the emotional support of my community.

18. I am open to expanding my network and meeting new people.

19. I am grateful for the sense of purpose I find in my community.

20. I am thankful for the experiences and perspectives of others.

21. I am open to embracing change with the support of my community.

Short Meditation

Title: Embracing Community

1. Find a quiet, comfortable place to sit and close your eyes.

2. Take several deep breaths, inhaling through your nose and exhaling through your mouth.

3. Bring your attention to the natural rhythm of your breath.

4. Silently repeat the affirmation: "I am grateful for my supportive community."

5. Visualize yourself surrounded by a circle of supportive and encouraging individuals. Feel a sense of connection and belonging.

6. As you breathe, your mind and body will be filled with gratitude and appreciation for your community.

7. Breathe deeply and repeat the affirmation for a few minutes.

8. When ready, gently open your eyes and return to the present moment.

Embracing Change:

The Spiritual Path to Personal Growth

Chapter 14: Spiritual Practices for Daily Life

Incorporating spiritual practices into our everyday lives helps us stay connected to our higher selves and navigate change with grace and wisdom. This chapter explores various spiritual practices and how they can be seamlessly integrated into our routines, supporting our spiritual growth and enhancing our overall well-being.

The Importance of Daily Spiritual Practices

Daily spiritual practices form a foundation for personal growth and transformation. They help cultivate mindfulness, deepen our connection with the divine, and maintain balance and harmony. Regular practice fosters resilience, clarity, and a profound sense of inner peace.

Benefits of Daily Spiritual Practices

Incorporating spiritual practices into our daily lives offers numerous benefits, including:

1. **Increased Mindfulness**: Spiritual practices help us remain present and fully engaged in our experiences, enhancing awareness and clarity.

2. **Enhanced Emotional Well-Being**: Consistent practice promotes emotional stability and reduces stress, anxiety, and negative feelings.

3. **Deeper Connection with the Divine**: Spiritual practices strengthen our bond with our higher selves and the divine, instilling a sense of purpose and meaning.

4. **Improved Mental Clarity**: Regular practice boosts our ability to focus, make decisions, and solve problems with greater insight and wisdom.

5. **Greater Inner Peace**: Spiritual practices nurture a sense of inner tranquility, enabling us to navigate life's challenges with grace and ease.

Spiritual Practices for Daily Life

Here are some spiritual practices you can easily incorporate into your daily routine to support your spiritual growth and overall well-being:

1. Meditation: Meditation is a powerful way to quiet the mind, cultivate inner peace, and connect with the divine. Dedicate time each day to meditate, focusing on your breath, a mantra, or a visualization.

2. Mindfulness: Practice mindfulness by staying present and fully immersed in your experiences. Pay attention to your thoughts, feelings, and sensations without judgment, and engage in mindful activities like eating, walking, or breathing.

3. Prayer: Prayer involves communicating with the divine, expressing gratitude, seeking guidance, and setting intentions.

Dedicate time each day for worship to connect with your higher self and the sacred.

4. Journaling: Journaling serves as a reflective practice that enables you to delve into your thoughts, feelings, and experiences. Use it to gain insights, establish intentions, and monitor your spiritual development.

5. Gratitude Practice: Foster a mindset of gratitude by consistently recognizing and valuing the positive aspects of your life. Maintain a gratitude journal, noting three things you appreciate each day.

6. Affirmations: Employ positive affirmations to strengthen a constructive mindset and align with your spiritual aspirations. Recite these affirmations daily to build self-confidence, resilience, and inner peace.

7. Yoga and Movement: Participate in yoga or similar mindful movement practices to connect with your body and enhance your physical and mental health. Yoga integrates physical postures, breathwork, and meditation to support overall well-being and spiritual development.

8. Breathwork: Utilize breathwork techniques to calm your mind, alleviate stress, and foster mindfulness. Methods such as diaphragmatic breathing, 4-7-8 breathing, and box breathing can be particularly effective.

9. Acts of Kindness: Engage in kind acts and service to others. Helping those in need cultivates a sense of connection, purpose, and fulfillment while aligning with spiritual principles of compassion and love.

10. Connecting with Nature: Spend time outdoors to reconnect with the natural rhythms of life and experience a sense of awe. Nature serves as a powerful teacher and healer on your spiritual path.

Practical Exercises for Daily Spiritual Practices

Here are some practical exercises to help integrate spiritual practices into your daily life:

1. Daily Meditation: Set aside time each day for meditation. Find a quiet space to sit comfortably, close your eyes, and focus on your breath or a mantra.

2. Mindful Breathing: Practice mindful breathing throughout the day. Take moments to concentrate on your breath, observing the rise and fall of your chest with each inhalation and exhalation.

3. Gratitude Journaling: Keep a gratitude journal, recording three things you are thankful for each day. Reflect on the positive elements of your life and the blessings you receive.

4. Positive Affirmations: Create a list of affirmations that resonate with you and repeat them daily to reinforce your spiritual goals.

5. Yoga Practice: Integrate yoga into your daily routine. Engage in physical postures, breathwork, and meditation to enhance your physical and mental health.

6. Acts of Kindness: Seek out opportunities to perform acts of kindness. Reflect on how these actions resonate with your spiritual values and create a sense of fulfillment.

7. Nature Walks: Spend time in nature, taking mindful walks to reconnect with the environment. Notice the beauty and rhythms of nature and contemplate the lessons it imparts.

Incorporating these practices into your daily routine can foster your spiritual growth, improve your well-being, and help you face life's challenges with grace and wisdom.

Affirmations

1. I am connected to my higher self and the divine.

2. I am grateful for my daily spiritual practice.

3. I am present and fully engaged in my experiences.

4. I am at peace with myself and the world around me.

5. I am open to the wisdom and guidance of the divine.

6. I am grateful for the inner peace and clarity I cultivate.

7. I am confident in my ability to navigate life's challenges.

8. I am thankful for the blessings and opportunities in my life.

9. I am open to the flow of positive energy and love.

10. I am committed to my spiritual growth and well-being.

11. I am grateful for the support of my spiritual practice.

12. I am focused on my spiritual goals and intentions.

13. I am at peace with the present moment.

14. I am open to new experiences and opportunities for growth.

15. I am thankful for the lessons and insights I gained.

16. I am confident in finding inner peace and balance.

17. I am grateful for the beauty and wonder of nature.

18. I am open to the flow of divine wisdom and guidance.

19. I am thankful for the love and support of my community.

20. I am committed to living a life of purpose and meaning.

21. I am grateful for my journey of spiritual growth.

Short Meditation

Title: Daily Spiritual Practice

1. Find a quiet, comfortable place to sit and close your eyes.

2. Take several deep breaths, inhaling through your nose and exhaling through your mouth.

3. Bring your attention to the natural rhythm of your breath.

4. Silently repeat the affirmation: "I am connected to my higher self and the divine."

5. Visualize yourself engaging in your daily spiritual practices, feeling a sense of peace and connection.

6. As you breathe, feel a sense of calm and clarity filling your mind and body.

7. Breathe deeply and repeat the affirmation for a few minutes.

8. When ready, gently open your eyes and return to the present moment.

Chapter 15: Integrating Change into Your Life

Integrating change into your life means accepting and adapting to new circumstances with grace and resilience. This chapter will discuss strategies for embracing change and seamlessly incorporating it into your growth journey, along with practical tools and techniques for transforming challenges into opportunities for development.

The Importance of Integrating Change

Change is an unavoidable part of life, and our ability to deal with change effectively determines our overall well-being and success. By accepting and incorporating change into our lives, we can confidently navigate transitions, maintain balance, and continue to grow and evolve.

Benefits of Integrating Change

Successfully incorporating change into your life can yield several advantages, such as:

1. **Increased Adaptability**: Welcoming change improves your capacity to adjust to new situations and environments with ease.

2. **Greater Resilience**: Embracing change fosters resilience, allowing you to recover from setbacks and challenges more effectively.

3. **Enhanced Personal Growth**: Accepting change promotes ongoing learning and personal development, helping you achieve your full potential.

4. **Improved Emotional Well-Being**: Effectively managing change can alleviate stress and anxiety, leading to greater emotional stability and well-being.

5. **Stronger Relationships**: Integrating change can enhance your relationships by nurturing empathy, communication, and mutual support.

Strategies for Integrating Change

Here are some approaches to help you integrate change into your life and turn challenges into growth opportunities:

1. **Embrace a Growth Mindset**: Foster a perspective that views change as a chance for growth and learning. Tackle challenges with curiosity and a willingness to adapt.

2. **Set Clear Intentions**: Clarify your goals and intentions regarding the change you want to integrate. Create a vision for how you plan to navigate new circumstances.

3. **Practice Mindfulness**: Engage in mindfulness to remain present and fully experience the process of change. This practice can help you manage stress and maintain balance.

4. **Develop a Support System**: Create a network of trusted friends, family, and mentors who can provide encouragement and guidance. Share your experiences and seek support as needed.

5. **Focus on Self-Care**: Make self-care a priority to maintain your physical, emotional, and mental well-being. Engage in activities that nourish your body and mind, like exercise, healthy eating, and relaxation techniques.

6. **Break Down Goals**: Divide your goals into manageable steps and celebrate your achievements. Setting small, attainable milestones can keep you motivated and focused.

7. **Reflect on Past Successes**: Consider past experiences where you successfully managed change. Use the lessons learned and strengths gained to guide you through current transitions.

8. **Stay Flexible and Open**: Be willing to adjust your approach and embrace new opportunities. Remain adaptable as circumstances change.

9. **Practice Gratitude**: Develop a gratitude mindset by focusing on the positive aspects of change. Appreciate the lessons and growth that arise from new experiences.

10. **Engage in Positive Self-Talk**: Utilize positive affirmations and constructive self-talk to nurture a positive mindset. Encourage yourself with affirmations that align with your goals and intentions.

Practical Exercises for Integrating Change

Here are some practical exercises to help you embrace change and transform challenges into growth opportunities:

1. **Vision Board Creation**: Design a vision board that illustrates your goals and aspirations related to change. Use inspiring images and words that motivate you.

2. **Mindfulness Meditation**: Practice mindfulness meditation to remain present and fully experience the change process. Concentrate on your breath and observe your thoughts without judgment.

3. **Goal Setting**: Write down your goals and break them into actionable steps. Create a timeline for achieving these goals and set milestones to track your progress.

4. **Gratitude Journaling**: Maintain a gratitude journal, noting three things you're thankful for each day. Reflect on the positive aspects of change and the blessings you receive.

5. **Positive Affirmations**: Compile a list of positive affirmations and recite them daily. Choose affirmations that resonate with you and reinforce your goals.

6. **Support System Check-In**: Regularly connect with your support system. Offer and seek support, share experiences, and stay in touch.

By incorporating these practices into your daily routine, you can effectively embrace change and turn challenges into opportunities for growth.

Affirmations

1. I am embracing change with grace and resilience.

2. I am open to new opportunities and experiences.

3. I am grateful for the growth that comes from change.

4. I am confident in my ability to navigate change.

5. I am thankful for the support and encouragement I received.

6. I am focused on my goals and intentions.

7. I am adaptable and open to adjustments.

8. I am grateful for the lessons and insights I gained.

9. I am at peace with the process of change.

10. I am committed to my personal growth and development.

11. I am confident in my ability to overcome challenges.

12. I am grateful for the positive aspects of change.

13. I am focused on creating a fulfilling and meaningful life.

14. I am open to positive energy flow in my life.

15. I am thankful for my journey of personal growth.

16. I am resilient and able to bounce back from setbacks.

17. I am grateful for my ability to adapt and thrive.

18. I am open to new possibilities and perspectives.

19. I am thankful for the progress I make each day.

20. I am confident in my path and direction.

21. I am at peace with the changes in my life.

Short Meditation

Title: Embracing Change

1. Find a quiet, comfortable place to sit and close your eyes.

2. Take several deep breaths, inhaling through your nose and exhaling through your mouth.

3. Bring your attention to the natural rhythm of your breath.

4. Silently repeat the affirmation: "I am embracing change with grace and resilience."

5. Visualize yourself navigating change confidently and efficiently, embracing new opportunities and experiences.

6. As you breathe, feel a sense of calm and clarity filling your mind and body.

7. Breathe deeply and repeat the affirmation for a few minutes.

8. When ready, gently open your eyes and return to the present moment.

Chapter 16: Embracing Change in Relationships

Relationships play a crucial role in our lives and are subject to change. This chapter discusses strategies for accepting change in relationships with family, friends, or romantic partners. We will explore how to navigate transitions, communicate effectively, and maintain healthy connections.

The Dynamics of Change in Relationships

Change is an inherent aspect of relationships as individuals grow and evolve. These shifts can involve changes in roles, responsibilities, interests, and circumstances. Embracing changes in relationships requires adapting to new dynamics and ensuring open communication to foster mutual understanding and support.

Benefits of Embracing Change in Relationships

Accepting change in relationships can lead to several benefits, including:

1. **Strengthened Connections**: Adapting together can deepen the bond between individuals, promoting greater understanding and empathy.

2. **Enhanced Communication**: Navigating change encourages transparent and honest communication, which is vital for healthy relationships.

3. **Personal Growth**: Accepting change fosters personal development as individuals learn to adjust and acquire new skills.

4. **Increased Resilience**: Successfully managing relationship changes enhances resilience, equipping individuals to face future challenges confidently.

5. **Greater Fulfillment**: Embracing change can lead to more satisfying and meaningful relationships as individuals align their connections with their evolving values and aspirations.

Strategies for Embracing Change in Relationships

Here are some strategies to help you accept change in relationships while maintaining strong, healthy connections:

1. **Communicate Openly**: Keep lines of communication open with your loved ones. Share your thoughts, feelings, and concerns, and encourage them to do the same.

2. **Listen Actively**: Engage in active listening by fully participating in conversations and demonstrating empathy. Validate the other person's feelings and perspectives.

3. **Set Boundaries**: Define clear boundaries to ensure mutual respect. Communicate your needs and expectations, and encourage others to express theirs

4. **Be Flexible**: Stay adaptable to change and be willing to adjust. Flexibility is crucial for navigating relationship shifts while maintaining harmony.

5. **Support Each Other**: Provide encouragement and support during times of transition. Be present for your loved ones and show that you care about their well-being.

6. **Reflect on Shared Goals**: Consider your common goals and values, discussing how changes may affect them. Work together to align your aspirations and create a shared vision for the future.

7. **Practice Patience**: Be patient with yourself and others while navigating change, recognizing that adjustments take time and effort.

8. **Seek Outside Help**: If necessary, consider consulting a therapist or counselor to assist with significant relationship changes. Professional guidance can offer valuable insights and strategies.

9. **Celebrate Milestones**: Acknowledge and celebrate milestones and achievements together. Recognize and appreciate the progress made as a team.

10. **Embrace Growth**: View changes in relationships as opportunities for growth. Welcome the chance to learn and evolve together.

Practical Exercises for Embracing Change in Relationships

Here are some practical exercises to help you accept change in relationships and maintain strong, healthy connections:

1. **Communication Check-In**: Schedule regular meetings to discuss your thoughts, feelings, and experiences, using this time to share openly and listen actively.

2. **Active Listening Practice**: Engage in conversations fully and show empathy, reflecting on the other person's words to ensure mutual understanding.

3. **Boundary Setting Exercise**: Take time to identify and communicate your boundaries to loved ones, encouraging them to share theirs as well.

4. **Shared Goals Discussion**: Talk about your shared goals and values with your loved ones, reflecting on how changes may impact these objectives and collaborating to align your vision for the future.

5. **Patience and Compassion Meditation**: Practice meditation focused on patience and compassion, visualizing yourself and your loved ones navigating change with understanding and support.

6. **Celebrating Milestones**: Create a list of shared milestones and achievements. Celebrate these moments and reflect on your collective progress.

Embracing Change:

The Spiritual Path to Personal Growth

Incorporating these exercises into your routine can help you embrace change in relationships and maintain strong, healthy connections.

Affirmations

1. I am open to change in my relationships.

2. I am grateful for the growth that comes from change.

3. I am committed to open and honest communication.

4. I am empathetic and understanding towards others.

5. I am patient and compassionate in my relationships.

6. I am flexible and adaptable to new dynamics.

7. I am supportive and encouraging towards my loved ones.

8. I am aligned with my shared goals and values.

9. I am grateful for the strong connections in my life.

10. I am confident in my ability to navigate change in relationships.

11. I am thankful for the progress and milestones we have achieved.

12. I am open to learning and evolving together.

13. I am grateful for the resilience we build together.

14. I am committed to maintaining healthy boundaries.

15. I am at peace with the changes in my relationships.

16. I am open to new opportunities for growth and connection.

17. I am grateful for the understanding and support I receive.

18. I am confident in our ability to handle challenges.

19. I am thankful for the harmony and balance in my relationships.

20. I am open to embracing change with grace and wisdom.

21. I am grateful for the love and connection in my life.

Short Meditation

Title: Embracing Change in Relationships

1. Find a quiet, comfortable place to sit and close your eyes.

2. Take several deep breaths, inhaling through your nose and exhaling through your mouth.

3. Bring your attention to the natural rhythm of your breath.

4. Silently repeat the affirmation: "I am open to change in my relationships."

5. Visualize yourself and your loved ones navigating change with empathy, understanding, and support.

6. As you breathe, feel a sense of connection and harmony filling your mind and body.

7. Breathe deeply and repeat the affirmation for a few minutes.

8. When ready, gently open your eyes and return to the present moment.

Chapter 17: Navigating Career Transitions

Career transitions represent significant changes that can affect various areas of our lives. This chapter discusses strategies for navigating these transitions, whether you're switching jobs, exploring new career paths, or adapting to changes in your current role. We will focus on approaching these transitions with confidence, resilience, and purpose.

The Impact of Career Transitions

Career transitions can present both opportunities and challenges. They often require leaving familiar roles behind and stepping into new, uncharted territory. Effectively navigating these transitions demands adaptability, a positive mindset, and a clear vision for the future.

Benefits of Successfully Navigating Career Transitions

Successfully managing career transitions can lead to various benefits, including:

1. **Professional Growth**: Transitions create chances to learn new skills, gain experience, and advance your career.

2. **Increased Fulfillment**: Pursuing a career aligned with your values and passions can enhance job satisfaction.

3. **Enhanced Resilience**: Navigating career changes builds resilience, allowing you to face future challenges with confidence.

4. **Expanded Network**: Transitions often involve meeting new people, and broadening your professional network.

5. **Personal Development**: Adapting to new roles fosters personal growth and self-discovery.

Strategies for Navigating Career Transitions

Here are some strategies to help you navigate career transitions with confidence and resilience:

1. **Clarify Your Goals**: Reflect on your career aspirations and identify what you want to achieve. Outline your long-term vision and the steps needed to reach it.

2. **Assess Your Skills and Strengths**: Evaluate your skills and experiences to see how they align with your career goals and can be utilized in new roles.

3. **Stay Informed and Prepared**: Research potential career paths and industries. Keep up with market trends, job requirements, and emerging fields.

4. **Seek Guidance and Support**: Connect with mentors, career coaches, and professional networks for advice and encouragement. Learn from those who have successfully navigated similar changes.

5. **Update Your Resume and Online Profiles**: Ensure that your resume and LinkedIn profile reflect your current skills, experiences, and career goals.

6. **Develop a Learning Plan**: Identify skill gaps and create a plan to address them, such as taking courses or obtaining certifications.

7. **Network Actively**: Participate in networking activities to connect with professionals in your desired field. Attend industry events and join professional organizations.

8. **Embrace Flexibility**: Stay open to new opportunities and be willing to adapt. Career transitions may not always follow a straight path, so flexibility is crucial.

9. **Practice Self-Care**: Prioritize your physical, emotional, and mental well-being through activities that nourish your body and mind, such as exercise and relaxation techniques.

10. **Cultivate a Positive Mindset**: Approach transitions with a positive attitude, focusing on growth and development opportunities rather than challenges.

Practical Exercises for Navigating Career Transitions

Here are some exercises to help you navigate career transitions with confidence and resilience:

Embracing Change:

The Spiritual Path to Personal Growth

1. **Goal Setting**: Write down your career goals and create an actionable plan. Break your goals into smaller steps and set timelines for achieving them.

2. **Skills Assessment**: Reflect on your skills and create a list of transferable abilities that can be applied to new opportunities.

3. **Networking Plan**: Develop a plan that includes attending industry events, joining professional organizations, and connecting with industry professionals.

4. **Learning Plan**: Identify knowledge gaps and research courses or certifications that can enhance your qualifications.

5. **Positive Affirmations**: Create a list of affirmations related to your career transition and repeat them daily to reinforce a positive mindset.

6. **Visualization**: Practice visualizing your successful navigation of the career transition, imagining yourself in your desired roles and achieving your goals.

7. **Resume and Profile Updates**: Review and update your resume and online profiles to ensure they reflect your current skills and career aspirations.

By incorporating these exercises into your routine, you can navigate career transitions with confidence, resilience, and purpose.

Affirmations

1. I am confident in my ability to navigate career transitions.

2. I am open to new opportunities and experiences.

3. I am grateful for the growth and development that come from change.

4. I can achieve my career goals.

5. I am thankful for the support and guidance I receive.

6. I am adaptable and open to new possibilities.

7. I am focused on my professional growth and success.

8. I am grateful for the skills and strengths I possess.

9. I am confident in my ability to learn and grow.

10. I am open to building new professional relationships.

11. I am grateful for the opportunities to expand my network.

12. I am focused on creating a fulfilling and meaningful career.

13. I am adaptable and resilient in the face of change.

14. I am thankful for the lessons and insights I gained from my experiences.

15. I am confident in my path and direction.

16. I am open to new perspectives and opportunities for growth.

17. I am grateful for the progress I make each day.

18. I am thankful for the clarity and direction in my career.

19. I am focused on achieving my professional aspirations.

20. I am open to the flow of positive energy and opportunities in my career.

21. I am grateful for my journey of professional growth.

Short Meditation

Title: Navigating Career Transitions

1. Find a quiet, comfortable place to sit and close your eyes.

2. Take several deep breaths, inhaling through your nose and exhaling through your mouth.

3. Bring your attention to the natural rhythm of your breath.

4. Silently repeat the affirmation: "I am confident in my ability to navigate career transitions."

5. Visualize yourself successfully navigating your career transition, achieving your goals, and experiencing fulfillment.

6. As you breathe, feel a sense of confidence and clarity filling your mind and body.

7. Breathe deeply and repeat the affirmation for a few minutes.

8. When ready, gently open your eyes and return to the present moment.

Chapter 18: Health and Well-Being During Change

Maintaining your health and well-being during periods of change is essential for navigating transitions with resilience and clarity. This chapter discusses strategies for prioritizing your physical, emotional, and mental health while adapting to new situations, highlighting the importance of self-care and practical ways to integrate healthy habits into your daily routine.

The Importance of Health and Well-Being

Health and well-being form the foundation of our overall quality of life. During times of change, prioritizing self-care is crucial for maintaining balance and stability. Caring for your health supports your ability to adapt, manage stress, and thrive through transitions.

Benefits of Prioritizing Health and Well-Being

Focusing on health and well-being during change can yield numerous advantages, including:

1. **Increased Resilience**: Good health strengthens your ability to recover from challenges.

2. **Improved Emotional Stability**: Prioritizing well-being helps regulate stress, anxiety, and emotional ups and downs.

3. **Enhanced Mental Clarity**: Healthy habits support cognitive function, leading to better decision-making and problem-solving.

4. **Greater Energy and Vitality**: Caring for your body provides the energy needed to navigate change and pursue goals.

5. **Overall Life Satisfaction**: Focusing on health and well-being contributes to increased happiness and fulfillment.

Strategies for Maintaining Health and Well-Being

Here are strategies to support your health and well-being during times of change:

1. **Prioritize Sleep**: Aim for 7-9 hours of quality sleep each night to bolster physical and mental health.

2. **Eat Nutritious Foods**: Focus on a balanced diet rich in fruits, vegetables, whole grains, lean proteins, and healthy fats to enhance overall well-being.

3. **Stay Hydrated**: Drink plenty of water throughout the day to maintain hydration, which is vital for physical and mental function.

4. **Exercise Regularly**: Engage in physical activities you enjoy to maintain fitness and reduce stress, such as walking, yoga, swimming, or dancing.

5. **Practice Mindfulness**: Incorporate mindfulness techniques into your daily routine to help manage stress and stay grounded during transitions.

6. **Connect with Loved Ones**: Maintain strong relationships with family and friends, as social support is crucial for emotional well-being.

7. **Manage Stress**: Use stress management techniques like deep breathing, meditation, or journaling to cope effectively.

8. **Take Breaks**: Allow time for rest and recharge; avoid overwhelming yourself with tasks and responsibilities.

9. **Set Realistic Goals**: Establish achievable goals and break them into manageable steps to prevent burnout.

10. **Seek Professional Help**: If needed, consult healthcare professionals or therapists for guidance and support in maintaining your well-being.

Practical Exercises for Health and Well-Being

Incorporate these practical exercises to prioritize your health and well-being during times of change:

Embracing Change:

The Spiritual Path to Personal Growth

1. **Sleep Hygiene Routine**: Develop a calming bedtime routine that promotes restful sleep, such as avoiding screens before bed and sticking to a regular schedule.

2. **Meal Planning**: Plan meals to ensure a balanced diet and prepare healthy snacks for convenience.

3. **Hydration Tracker**: Use a tracker to monitor your water intake and set reminders to drink water throughout the day.

4. **Exercise Schedule**: Create a plan for regular physical activity, aiming for at least 30 minutes most days.

5. **Mindfulness Practice**: Dedicate time each day to mindfulness activities, such as focusing on your breath or guided meditation.

6. **Social Connection Plan**: Schedule regular check-ins with loved ones and engage in social activities that bring joy.

7. **Stress Management Toolkit**: Build a toolkit of stress relief techniques, including deep breathing and creative expression.

8. **Breaks and Rest**: Include regular breaks in your day to relax and recharge.

9. **Goal Setting Exercise**: Write down your goals in actionable steps, establish a timeline, and celebrate your progress.

10. **Professional Support**: Consider consulting healthcare professionals for expert guidance on maintaining well-being.

By incorporating these exercises into your routine, you can prioritize health and well-being during times of change and navigate transitions with resilience and clarity.

Affirmations

1. I am prioritizing my health and well-being.

2. I am grateful for my body and its ability to heal.

3. I am open to nourishing my mind, body, and spirit.

4. I am committed to self-care and wellness.

5. I am thankful for the support of my loved ones.

6. I am focused on maintaining a balanced and healthy lifestyle.

7. I am confident in my ability to manage stress.

8. I am grateful for the energy and vitality I have.

9. I am open to new opportunities for growth and well-being.

10. I am thankful for the progress I make each day.

11. I am committed to getting adequate sleep and rest.

12. I am grateful for the nutritious foods that fuel my body.

13. I am focused on staying hydrated and healthy.

14. I am confident in my ability to prioritize self-care.

15. I am thankful for the strength and resilience within me.

16. I am open to connecting with my loved ones.

17. I am grateful for the support and guidance I receive.

18. I am focused on creating a fulfilling and balanced life.

19. I am open to the flow of positive energy and health.

20. I am committed to my journey of wellness and growth.

21. I am thankful for the well-being and harmony in my life.

Short Meditation

Title: Prioritizing Health and Well-Being

1. Find a quiet, comfortable place to sit and close your eyes.

2. Take several deep breaths, inhaling through your nose and exhaling through your mouth.

3. Bring your attention to the natural rhythm of your breath.

4. Silently repeat the affirmation: "I prioritize my health and well-being."

5. Visualize yourself engaging in healthy habits, such as eating nutritious foods, exercising, and practicing mindfulness.

6. As you breathe, feel a sense of vitality and well-being filling your mind and body.

7. Breathe deeply and repeat the affirmation for a few minutes.

8. When ready, gently open your eyes and return to the present moment.

Chapter 19: Embracing Change with a Positive Mindset

A positive mindset is vital for effectively managing change. In this chapter, we will explore the transformative power of positive thinking and discuss strategies for cultivating an optimistic outlook, including reframing negative thoughts, practicing gratitude, and focusing on solutions.

The Power of Positive Thinking

Positive thinking means emphasizing the good aspects of situations and maintaining an optimistic perspective. It does not imply ignoring challenges but rather facing them with a constructive and hopeful attitude. Adopting a positive mindset can significantly enhance our ability to adapt to change and uncover growth opportunities.

Benefits of a Positive Mindset

Embracing a positive mindset during periods of change can yield several benefits, such as:

1. **Increased Resilience**: Positive thinking helps us recover from setbacks more easily.

2. **Improved Mental Health**: A positive attitude can lower stress, anxiety, and negative emotions, enhancing overall mental well-being.

3. **Enhanced Problem-Solving Skills**: By concentrating on solutions rather than problems, we can find creative and effective ways to tackle challenges.

4. **Greater Motivation**: Optimism boosts our drive and motivation to achieve our goals.

5. **Better Relationships**: A positive outlook fosters empathy, compassion, and effective communication, strengthening connections with others.

Strategies for Cultivating a Positive Mindset

Here are strategies to help you develop a positive mindset and embrace change with optimism:

1. **Reframe Negative Thoughts**: Challenge negative thinking by focusing on the positives. Replace negative self-talk with positive affirmations.

2. **Practice Gratitude**: Regularly acknowledge the good in your life by keeping a gratitude journal and noting three things you're thankful for each day.

3. **Focus on Solutions**: When facing challenges, direct your attention toward finding solutions instead of dwelling on problems.

4. **Visualize Success**: Use visualization to imagine positive outcomes. Picture yourself achieving goals and handling change with confidence.

5. **Surround Yourself with Positivity**: Seek uplifting influences, including supportive friends and inspiring media, while minimizing exposure to negativity.

6. **Engage in Positive Activities**: Participate in hobbies, exercise, and creative pursuits that bring joy and reinforce a positive mindset.

7. **Set Realistic Goals**: Create achievable goals and celebrate your progress. Break larger goals into smaller, manageable steps.

8. **Use Positive Affirmations**: Repeat affirmations daily to strengthen a positive mindset and build self-confidence.

9. **Practice Self-Compassion**: Be kind to yourself, especially during challenging times. Recognize your efforts and strengths.

10. **Connect with Positive People**: Foster relationships with those who inspire and support your growth.

Practical Exercises for Cultivating a Positive Mindset

Here are exercises to help you nurture a positive mindset:

1. **Gratitude Journaling**: Maintain a journal to note three things you are grateful for each day, reflecting on the positive aspects of your life.

2. **Positive Affirmations**: Develop a list of affirmations that resonate with you and repeat them daily to reinforce your goals and values.

3. **Visualization**: Practice visualizing positive outcomes and success, seeing yourself achieve your goals confidently.

4. **Reframing**: Challenge and reframe negative thoughts by finding evidence that contradicts them and replacing them with constructive ideas.

5. **Mindfulness Meditation**: Engage in mindfulness meditation to enhance awareness of your thoughts and emotions, cultivating calm and clarity.

6. **Positive Activities**: Dedicate time to activities that bring joy, such as hobbies and exercise, to boost your mood and reinforce positivity.

By incorporating these exercises into your daily routine, you can cultivate a positive mindset and embrace change with resilience and optimism.

Affirmations

1. I am embracing change with a positive mindset.

2. I am grateful for the opportunities that change brings.

3. I am confident in my ability to navigate change.

4. I am focused on finding solutions to challenges.

5. I am grateful for my inner strength and resilience.

6. I am optimistic about the future.

7. I am thankful for the support of my loved ones.

8. I am confident in my ability to achieve my goals.

9. I am grateful for the lessons that challenges teach me.

10. I am focused on the positive aspects of every situation.

11. I am open to new possibilities and experiences.

12. I am thankful for the growth that comes from change.

13. I am confident in my ability to adapt and thrive.

14. I am grateful for the joy and fulfillment in my life.

15. I am optimistic and proactive in my approach to challenges.

16. I am thankful for the support and encouragement I received.

17. I am confident in my ability to overcome obstacles.

18. I am grateful for the opportunities for growth and improvement.

19. I am focused on the present moment and its blessings.

20. I am open to positive energy flow in my life.

21. I am grateful for my positive mindset and outlook.

Short Meditation

Title: Embracing Change with a Positive Mindset

1. Find a quiet, comfortable place to sit and close your eyes.

2. Take several deep breaths, inhaling through your nose and exhaling through your mouth.

3. Bring your attention to the natural rhythm of your breath.

4. Silently repeat the affirmation: "I am embracing change with a positive mindset."

5. Visualize yourself navigating change with optimism and confidence, focusing on the positive aspects and opportunities for growth.

6. As you breathe, feel a sense of positivity and optimism filling your mind and body.

7. Breathe deeply and repeat the affirmation for a few minutes.

8. When ready, gently open your eyes and return to the present moment.

Chapter 20: Developing Intuition and Inner Guidance

Developing intuition and inner guidance is essential for making informed decisions and confidently navigating change. This chapter delves into the nature of intuition, its benefits, and practical strategies for enhancing your connection to inner wisdom. We will explore how intuition can assist you through life's transitions and support your spiritual growth.

The Nature of Intuition

Intuition is often described as a gut feeling or inner knowing that guides our decisions. It transcends rational thought and logic, providing insights and clarity that align our choices with our true selves and higher purpose.

Benefits of Developing Intuition

Cultivating intuition offers numerous advantages, particularly during periods of change, including:

1. **Enhanced Decision-Making**: Intuition aids in making choices that align with your authentic self.

2. **Increased Confidence**: Trusting your intuition boosts self-confidence and reduces doubt.

3. **Greater Clarity**: Intuition provides perspective, helping you understand complex situations.

4. **Improved Problem-Solving**: Intuitive insights can lead to creative solutions for challenges.

5. **Deepened Spiritual Connection**: Developing intuition strengthens your bond with your higher self and the divine, fostering spiritual growth.

Strategies for Developing Intuition

Here are strategies to enhance your intuition and inner guidance:

1. **Practice Mindfulness**: Mindfulness quiets the mind and heightens awareness, making it easier to tune into intuitive insights through meditation and deep breathing.

2. **Listen to Your Body**: Pay attention to physical sensations and emotions when making decisions; your body often signals intuitive guidance.

3. **Trust Your Gut Feelings**: Recognize and follow your gut feelings; they can provide valuable direction.

4. **Reflect and Journal**: Dedicate time for self-reflection and journaling, exploring thoughts and any intuitive insights that emerge.

5. **Practice Visualization**: Visualize making decisions and taking actions that align with your intuition to enhance your connection to inner wisdom.

6. **Spend Time in Nature**: Nature promotes intuition by providing a calm environment, allowing you to connect with the natural world.

7. **Engage in Creative Activities**: Pursue creative outlets like painting or writing, which can help unlock intuitive insights.

8. **Seek Solitude**: Spend time alone to connect with your inner self and listen to your intuition without distractions.

9. **Meditate on Intuition**: Use guided meditations focused on intuition to strengthen your intuitive abilities.

10. **Practice Patience**: Developing intuition requires time and practice, so be patient and trust the process.

Practical Exercises for Developing Intuition

Here are exercises to enhance your intuition and inner guidance:

1. **Mindfulness Meditation**: Dedicate daily time to mindfulness meditation, focusing on your breath while observing thoughts and feelings without judgment.

2. **Intuitive Journaling**: Keep a journal to document intuitive insights related to decisions and actions.

3. **Visualization Practice**: Utilize visualization techniques to connect with your inner wisdom and envision making aligned decisions.

4. **Nature Walks**: Spend time outdoors to heighten your intuitive abilities by connecting with the environment.

5. **Creative Expression**: Engage in creative activities to allow your intuition to emerge without judgment.

6. **Solitude Practice**: Take time for quiet reflection, listening to your inner self and intuition.

7. **Guided Meditation**: Use guided meditations designed to develop intuition, following prompts to connect with your inner wisdom.

8. **Body Awareness**: Notice physical sensations and emotions that arise during decision-making, paying attention to gut feelings.

9. ** Patience and Trust**: Practice patience and trust in developing your intuition. Allow yourself to develop and progress at your own pace.

By incorporating these exercises into your routine, you can develop your intuition and inner guidance, aiding you in navigating change with confidence and clarity.

Affirmations

1. I am connected to my inner wisdom and intuition.

2. I am confident in my ability to make intuitive decisions.

3. I am grateful for the guidance of my higher self.

4. I am open to receiving intuitive insights and clarity.

5. I am thankful for the inner knowing that guides me.

6. I am trusting my gut feelings and inner nudges.

7. I am open to the flow of intuitive wisdom.

8. I am grateful for the clarity and perspective I receive.

9. I am confident in my ability to navigate change with intuition.

10. I am thankful for the guidance and support of the divine.

11. I am open to the wisdom of my body and emotions.

12. I am grateful for the intuitive signals that guide my choices.

13. I am confident in my ability to find creative solutions.

14. I am open to the insights and guidance of my higher self.

15. I am thankful for the clarity and understanding I gained.

16. I am trusting the process of developing my intuition.

17. I am open to new opportunities for growth and guidance.

18. I am grateful for the inner peace and confidence I feel.

19. I am confident in my path and direction.

20. I am open to the flow of intuitive energy in my life.

21. I am grateful for my journey of intuition and inner growth.

Short Meditation

Title: Developing Intuition and Inner Guidance

1. Find a quiet, comfortable place to sit and close your eyes.

2. Take several deep breaths, inhaling through your nose and exhaling through your mouth.

3. Bring your attention to the natural rhythm of your breath.

4. Silently repeat the affirmation: "I am connected to my inner wisdom and intuition."

5. Visualize yourself making decisions and taking actions that align with your intuition. Feel the confidence and clarity that come from trusting your inner guidance.

6. As you breathe, feel a sense of connection and wisdom filling your mind and body.

7. Breathe deeply and repeat the affirmation for a few minutes.

8. When ready, gently open your eyes and return to the present moment.

Chapter 21: The Power of Affirmations

Affirmations are powerful tools for transforming our mindset and facilitating positive changes in our lives. In this chapter, we will examine what affirmations are, their benefits, and how to effectively integrate them into your daily routine. We will discuss how affirmations can assist in navigating change, enhancing self-confidence, and aligning with your highest potential.

The Concept of Affirmations

Affirmations are positive statements designed to reinforce desired beliefs and outcomes. They help reprogram the subconscious mind by replacing negative thought patterns with empowering ones. By consistently repeating affirmations, we can shift our mindset and lay a positive foundation for personal growth and transformation.

Benefits of Using Affirmations

Regular use of affirmations can yield various benefits, particularly during times of change, such as:

1. **Increased Self-Confidence**: Affirmations enhance self-esteem and confidence by reinforcing positive self-beliefs.

2. **Improved Mental Clarity**: They help clear mental clutter and direct focus toward desired outcomes.

3. **Enhanced Resilience**: Affirmations foster mental resilience, allowing us to better cope with challenges.

4. **Greater Motivation**: Repeating affirmations boosts motivation and commitment to achieving our goals.

5. **Positive Mindset**: They promote a positive mindset, contributing to overall emotional well-being and happiness.

Strategies for Using Affirmations

Here are some effective strategies for utilizing affirmations to navigate change and achieve your goals:

1. **Choose Positive and Specific Statements**: Select affirmations that are positive, specific, and relevant to your goals. Use present tense and language that resonates with you.

2. **Repeat Daily**: Consistency is key. Repeat your affirmations daily, ideally in the morning and before bed, to reinforce the desired beliefs and outcomes.

3. **Visualize the Outcome**: As you recite affirmations, visualize yourself achieving the desired outcome, immersing yourself in the associated feelings, sights, and sounds.

4. **Write Them Down**: Record affirmations in a journal or on sticky notes around your home or workspace. Writing them down reinforces the messages and keeps them top of the mind.

5. **Say Them Aloud**: Speaking affirmations aloud adds another layer of reinforcement. Use a confident tone to empower your statements.

6. **Use Affirmation Apps**: Take advantage of apps that provide daily affirmations and reminders to help you maintain consistency.

7. **Combine with Meditation**: Integrate affirmations into your meditation practice, repeating them silently or aloud to deepen their impact.

8. **Personalize Your Affirmations**: Tailor affirmations to reflect your unique goals, values, and aspirations for greater meaning and effectiveness.

9. **Stay Patient and Persistent**: Change takes time. Be patient and persistent in your practice, and you will gradually notice shifts in your mindset and behavior.

Practical Exercises for Using Affirmations

Here are some practical exercises to incorporate affirmations into your daily life:

1. **Morning Affirmation Ritual**: Begin your day with a morning affirmation ritual by repeating your affirmations while looking in the mirror.

2. **Affirmation Journal**: Maintain an affirmation journal where you write down your affirmations daily and reflect on how they make you feel.

3. **Visualization Exercise**: Combine affirmations with visualization; close your eyes, repeat your affirmations, and envision yourself achieving your goals.

4. **Affirmation Cards**: Create cards with positive statements and place them in visible locations like your desk or mirror.

5. **Meditation with Affirmations**: Use meditation to repeat your affirmations, either silently or aloud, while in a meditative state.

6. **Evening Affirmation Ritual**: Conclude your day with an evening affirmation ritual, reflecting on your affirmations and their impact on your day.

7. **Affirmation Reminders**: Set reminders on your phone or utilize affirmation apps for daily positive statements.

8. **Group Affirmation Practice**: Share affirmations with friends or a group to support each other in reinforcing positive beliefs.

By incorporating these exercises into your daily routine, you can effectively use affirmations to navigate change, boost self-confidence, and align with your highest potential.

Affirmations

1. I am confident in my ability to navigate change.

2. I am grateful for the opportunities that come my way.

3. I am open to new experiences and growth.

4. I am strong, resilient, and capable.

5. I am worthy of success and happiness.

6. I am focused on my goals and dreams.

7. I am grateful for the support of my loved ones.

8. I am at peace with myself and my journey.

9. I am confident in my ability to achieve my goals.

10. I am open to the abundance of the universe.

11. I am thankful for my inner strength and wisdom.

12. I am optimistic about my future.

13. I am worthy of love and respect.

14. I am committed to my personal growth and development.

15. I am open to positive energy flow in my life.

16. I am grateful for the lessons and experiences that have shaped me.

17. I am confident in my ability to overcome challenges.

18. I am thankful for the progress I make each day.

19. I am focused on creating a fulfilling and meaningful life.

20. I am open to new possibilities and opportunities.

21. I am grateful for my journey of personal growth.

Short Meditation

Title: Embracing Affirmations

1. Find a quiet, comfortable place to sit and close your eyes.

2. Take several deep breaths, inhaling through your nose and exhaling through your mouth.

3. Bring your attention to the natural rhythm of your breath.

4. Silently repeat the affirmation: "I am confident in my ability to navigate change."

5. Visualize yourself achieving your goals and navigating change confidently and efficiently.

6. As you breathe, feel a sense of confidence and positivity filling your mind and body.

7. Breathe deeply and repeat the affirmation for a few minutes.

8. When ready, gently open your eyes and return to the present moment.

Chapter 22: Spirituality and Personal Growth

Spirituality is crucial in personal growth, providing a deeper sense of meaning, purpose, and connection. This chapter examines the link between spirituality and personal development, highlighting how spiritual practices can enhance your journey. We will also offer practical strategies for incorporating spirituality into your everyday life.

The Role of Spirituality in Personal Growth

Spirituality involves seeking a connection with something greater than ourselves, be it a higher power, the universe, or our inner wisdom. It offers a framework for understanding our place in the world and guides us as we face life's challenges and changes.

Benefits of Spirituality for Personal Growth

Integrating spirituality into your growth journey can yield various benefits, including:

1. **Greater Sense of Purpose**: Spirituality helps us discover our purpose and align our actions with our core values.

2. **Enhanced Resilience**: Spiritual practices offer strength and comfort during tough times, helping us remain resilient and hopeful.

3. **Increased Inner Peace**: Connecting with our spiritual selves promotes tranquility, reducing stress and anxiety.

4. **Deeper Self-Awareness**: Spirituality encourages introspection, leading to enhanced self-awareness and understanding.

5. **Stronger Connections**: Spirituality fosters empathy and compassion, enriching our relationships with others.

Strategies for Integrating Spirituality into Daily Life

Here are practical strategies for weaving spirituality into your daily routine to support personal growth:

1. **Establish a Spiritual Practice**: Develop a regular practice that resonates with you, such as meditation, prayer, or journaling.

2. **Reflect on Your Beliefs and Values**: Consider how your core beliefs guide your actions and decisions, aligning them with your spiritual journey.

3. **Seek Spiritual Community**: Connect with a community that shares your beliefs for support and a sense of belonging.

4. **Practice Mindfulness**: Incorporate mindfulness to stay present and connected to yourself and the world around you.

5. **Engage in Acts of Service**: Perform kind acts for others to foster a sense of purpose and connection.

6. **Read Spiritual Texts**: Explore literature that inspires and guides you on your spiritual path.

7. **Spend Time in Nature**: Appreciate the beauty of the natural world, which can serve as a source of spiritual inspiration.

8. **Practice Gratitude**: Regularly acknowledge the positive aspects of your life, a practice common in many spiritual traditions.

9. **Set Intentions**: Define clear intentions for your spiritual growth and reflect on how to align your actions with these goals.

10. **Meditate on Spiritual Principles**: Use meditation to connect with concepts like love and compassion, reflecting on how they guide your actions.

Practical Exercises for Spirituality and Personal Growth

To help integrate spirituality into your life, consider these exercises:

1. **Daily Meditation**: Dedicate time each day to meditate, focusing on your breath or a spiritual concept.

2. **Spiritual Journaling**: Keep a journal reflecting on your spiritual journey and insights gained.

3. **Acts of Service**: Engage in community service, aligning your actions with your spiritual values.

4. **Mindfulness Practice**: Stay present by focusing on your breath, thoughts, and surroundings.

5. **Nature Walks**: Spend time outdoors to connect with nature and reflect on its interconnectedness.

6. Gratitude Practice: Keep a gratitude journal and list three things you are grateful for daily. Reflect on how gratitude improves your spiritual well-being.

7. Reading Spiritual Texts: Schedule time to read spiritual books. Reflect on the teachings and how they apply to your life.

8. Community Involvement: Join a spiritual community or group that shares similar beliefs and values. Participate in activities, discussions, and events that promote spiritual growth.

9. Setting Intentions: Set clear goals for your spiritual growth. Think about your goals and how you can align your actions with your spiritual path.

10. Meditation on Spiritual Principles: Use meditation to connect with spiritual values like love, compassion, and forgiveness. Reflect on how these principles shape your actions and decisions.

By incorporating these exercises into your routine, you can deepen your spiritual journey and navigate life with purpose and peace.

Affirmations

1. I am connected to my higher self and the divine.

2. I am grateful for the guidance and support I receive.

3. I am open to spiritual growth and transformation.

4. I am at peace with myself and the world around me.

5. I am thankful for the sense of purpose in my life.

6. I am open to the flow of positive energy and love.

7. I am confident in my spiritual path and direction.

8. I am grateful for the strength and resilience within me.

9. I am connected to the beauty and wisdom of nature.

10. I am thankful for the support of my spiritual community.

11. I am focused on my spiritual growth and well-being.

12. I am open to new insights and understanding.

13. I am grateful for the inner peace and clarity I cultivate.

14. I am confident in my ability to navigate life's changes.

15. I am thankful for the lessons and experiences that have shaped me.

16. I am open to acts of kindness and service.

17. I am grateful for the love and compassion in my life.

18. I am focused on creating a fulfilling and meaningful life.

19. I am open to the flow of divine wisdom and guidance.

20. I am committed to my journey of spiritual growth.

21. I am grateful for my connection to something greater than myself.

Short Meditation

Title: Embracing Spiritual Growth

1. Find a quiet, comfortable place to sit and close your eyes.

2. Take several deep breaths, inhaling through your nose and exhaling through your mouth.

3. Bring your attention to the natural rhythm of your breath.

4. Silently repeat the affirmation: "I am connected to my higher self and the divine."

5. Visualize yourself growing spiritually, connecting with your inner wisdom and the divine.

6. Feel a sense of peace and connection filling your mind and body as you breathe.

7. Breathe deeply and repeat the affirmation for a few minutes.

8. When ready, gently open your eyes and return to the present moment.

Chapter 23: The Art of Letting Go

Letting go is crucial for embracing change and moving forward in life. This chapter delves into the art of letting go, its importance, and how it can foster personal growth and freedom. We will discuss practical strategies for releasing attachments, past experiences, and negative emotions that hold us back.

The Significance of Letting Go

Letting go involves releasing our attachment to things that no longer serve us, including past experiences and limiting beliefs. It means accepting life's transient nature and embracing change with an open heart. This process frees us from emotional baggage, creating space for new opportunities.

Benefits of Letting Go

The benefits of letting go, especially during times of change, include:

1. **Emotional Freedom**: Releasing attachments allows for greater peace and happiness.

2. **Improved Relationships**: Letting go of past grievances fosters forgiveness and empathy in our relationships.

3. **Increased Self-Esteem**: Recognizing our worth boosts our confidence and self-esteem.

4. **Enhanced Focus and Clarity**: Moving on from the past helps us concentrate on the present and make conscious choices.

5. **Greater Resilience**: Letting go builds resilience, enabling us to adapt to change.

Strategies for Letting Go

Here are strategies for embracing change and letting go:

1. **Acknowledge Your Emotions**: Validate your feelings about past experiences and process them without judgment.

2. **Practice Forgiveness**: Forgive yourself and others, releasing resentment and allowing yourself to move forward.

3. **Reflect on Lessons Learned**: Consider the insights gained from past experiences and how they contribute to your growth.

4. **Create a Letting Go Ritual**: Symbolically release the past by writing down grievances and discarding them.

5. **Focus on the Present**: Engage in mindfulness to fully experience the current moment.

6. **Set Intentions for the Future**: Define clear intentions for your future that align with your values.

7. **Seek Support**: Reach out to friends or support groups for encouragement and guidance.

8. **Engage in Self-Care**: Take care of your well-being through nourishing activities.

9. **Practice Gratitude**: Cultivate gratitude for the positive aspects of your life.

10. **Embrace Change**: View change as an opportunity for growth.

Practical Exercises for Letting Go

Here are practical exercises to help you release the past and embrace change:

1. **Journaling**: Write about past experiences and reflect on the lessons learned.

2. **Forgiveness Meditation**: Visualize forgiving yourself and others to release resentment.

3. **Letting Go Ritual**: Write down grievances and symbolically release them through a ritual.

4. **Mindfulness Practice**: Stay present by focusing on your breath and surroundings.

5. **Vision Board**: Create a vision board to represent your future goals and aspirations.

By incorporating these exercises, you can let go of the past and embrace change with freedom and possibility.

Affirmations

1. I am letting go of the past.

2. I am grateful for the lessons of my past experiences.

3. I am open to new possibilities and opportunities.

4. I am forgiving myself and others for past mistakes.

5. I am free from emotional burdens.

6. I am focused on the present moment.

7. I am grateful for my ability to move forward.

8. I am open to the flow of life and its changes.

9. I am thankful for the growth that comes from letting go.

10. I am confident in my ability to embrace change.

11. I am at peace with my past.

12. I am open to new experiences and relationships.

13. I am grateful for the wisdom gained from past experiences.

14. I am free to create a new future.

15. I am focused on my goals and aspirations.

16. I am grateful for the support of my loved ones.

17. I am at peace with the present moment.

18. I am open to opportunities for growth and improvement.

19. I am confident in my ability to adapt and thrive.

20. I am thankful for the journey of personal growth.

21. I am free to live my life fully and authentically.

Short Meditation

Title: Letting Go of the Past

1. Find a quiet place to sit comfortably and close your eyes.

2. Take several deep breaths, inhaling through your nose and exhaling through your mouth.

3. Bring your attention to the natural rhythm of your breath.

4. Silently repeat the affirmation: "I am letting go of the past."

5. Visualize yourself, releasing past experiences, regrets, and resentments. See them floating away, leaving you feeling lighter and more accessible.

6. Feel a sense of peace and freedom filling your mind and body as you breathe.

7. Breathe deeply and repeat the affirmation for a few minutes.

8. When ready, gently open your eyes and return to the present moment.

Chapter 24: Embracing Change Through Creativity

Creativity is a vital resource for managing change and expressing our true selves. This chapter discusses how embracing creativity can help us adapt to new situations, promote personal development, and improve our overall well-being. We will highlight the advantages of creative expression and offer practical strategies for weaving creativity into your daily life.

The Role of Creativity in Embracing Change

Creativity empowers us to explore different viewpoints, tackle problems in novel ways, and articulate our feelings. It helps us overcome limiting beliefs and envision new opportunities. In times of change, engaging with creativity can provide a sense of control, inspiration, and joy.

Benefits of Embracing Creativity

Incorporating creativity into your life, especially during transitions, can yield numerous benefits, including:

1. **Enhanced Problem-Solving Skills**: Creative thinking enables us to tackle challenges from new angles and discover innovative solutions.

2. **Increased Resilience**: Creative activities help us manage stress and build resilience by offering an emotional outlet and a sense of achievement.

3. **Improved Emotional Well-Being**: Creative expression allows us to process and release feelings, fostering mental and emotional health.

4. **Greater Self-Awareness**: Engaging in creative endeavors promotes self-reflection and deeper self-understanding.

5. **Boosted Confidence**: Creating something unique enhances self-esteem and personal confidence.

Strategies for Embracing Creativity

Here are some strategies to integrate creativity into your daily routine:

1. **Explore Various Creative Outlets**: Try different forms of creative expression, such as painting, writing, music, dance, photography, or crafts. Discover what resonates with you and brings you joy.

2. **Create a Dedicated Space**: Designate a distraction-free area in your home for creative activities. A dedicated space can inspire and motivate your creativity.

3. **Make Time for Creativity**: Schedule regular creative time in your daily or weekly calendar. Consistency is key to developing a creative practice.

4. **Embrace Imperfection**: Allow yourself to create without self-judgment or the pursuit of perfection. Focus on the process and enjoy the act of creating.

5. **Seek Inspiration**: Surround yourself with inspirational sources like nature, art, literature, music, and inspiring people. Inspiration can ignite new ideas and fuel your creativity.

6. **Collaborate with Others**: Engage in joint creative projects with friends, family, or community members. Collaboration can introduce fresh perspectives and enrich your creative experience.

7. **Use Creativity for Problem-Solving**: Apply creative thinking to everyday challenges. Brainstorm innovative solutions and approach situations with an open mind.

8. **Keep a Creative Journal**: Maintain a journal to capture your creative ideas, thoughts, and inspirations. Use it for brainstorming, sketching, or planning projects.

9. **Attend Workshops and Classes**: Participate in workshops or online courses to learn new creative skills and techniques, expanding your creative horizons.

10. **Practice Mindfulness**: Incorporate mindfulness into your creative endeavors. Stay present in the moment, fully engage in the creative process, and minimize distractions.

Practical Exercises for Embracing Creativity

Here are some exercises to help you cultivate creativity in your life:

1. **Creative Journaling**: Keep a journal for creative expression. Use it to write, draw, or brainstorm, reflecting on your creative journey and insights.

2. **Daily Creativity Time**: Dedicate 15-30 minutes each day to a creative activity. Experiment freely with different forms of expression.

3. **Mindful Creativity**: Focus on your senses and the materials you're using during a creative activity, engaging fully at the moment.

4. **Nature Inspiration**: Spend time outdoors and let nature inspire your creative work, whether through photography, painting, or writing.

5. **Creative Collaboration**: Team up with someone to work on a creative project. Share ideas and collaborate on the creative process.

6. **Art and Music Exploration**: Delve into various art forms and music genres. Visit galleries, attend concerts, or listen to new music to spark creativity.

7. **Vision Board Creation**: Assemble a vision board reflecting your goals and aspirations, using images and words that motivate you.

8. **Creative Challenges**: Participate in creative prompts or challenges that provide structure and inspiration for your creative practice.

9. **Learning New Skills**: Enroll in classes to acquire new creative skills, such as painting, pottery, or photography.

10. **Creative Breaks**: Integrate short creative breaks throughout your day for quick activities like doodling or writing.

By incorporating these exercises into your routine, you can harness creativity to navigate change, support personal growth, and enhance your overall well-being.

Affirmations

1. I am open to new creative possibilities.

2. I am confident in my ability to express myself creatively.

3. I am grateful for the joy and inspiration that creativity brings.

4. I am open to exploring different forms of creative expression.

5. I am confident in my ability to solve problems creatively.

6. I am grateful for the opportunity to learn and grow through creativity.

7. I am open to collaboration and sharing creative ideas.

8. I am confident in my unique creative voice.

9. I am grateful for the beauty and inspiration of the natural world.

10. I am open to the flow of creative energy in my life.

11. I am confident in my ability to embrace change through creativity.

12. I am grateful for the inner peace and well-being that creativity brings.

13. I am open to new sources of inspiration and ideas.

14. I am confident in my ability to create something meaningful.

15. I am grateful for the support and encouragement of my creative community.

16. I am open to the process of creative exploration and discovery.

17. I am confident in using creativity for personal growth.

18. I am grateful for the resilience and strength that creativity provides.

19. I am open to new experiences and creative challenges.

20. I am confident in integrating creativity into my daily life.

21. I am grateful for the fulfillment and satisfaction that creativity brings.

Short Meditation

Title: Embracing Creativity

1. Find a quiet, comfortable place to sit and close your eyes.

2. Take several deep breaths, inhaling through your nose and exhaling through your mouth.

3. Bring your attention to the natural rhythm of your breath.

4. Silently repeat the affirmation: "I am open to new creative possibilities."

5. Visualize yourself engaging in a creative activity, feeling inspired and joyful.

6. As you breathe, feel a sense of creative energy and inspiration filling your mind and body.

7. Continue to breathe deeply and repeat the affirmation for a few minutes.

8. When ready, gently open your eyes and return to the present moment.

Chapter 25: Building Resilience in the Face of Change

Resilience is the ability to adapt and thrive in times of adversity and change. This chapter examines the significance of building resilience, its advantages, and practical methods for cultivating a resilient mindset. We will explore how resilience enables us to tackle life's challenges and emerge stronger and more capable.

The Importance of Resilience

Resilience helps us manage stress, recover from setbacks, and maintain a positive outlook during tough times. It is an essential skill for personal development and well-being, empowering us to confront challenges with confidence and determination. By building resilience, we can adapt to change and turn obstacles into opportunities for growth.

Benefits of Building Resilience

Developing resilience offers many advantages, especially when facing change. These benefits include:

1. **Increased Adaptability**: Resilience enhances our capacity to adjust to new situations, making it easier to navigate transitions.

2. **Improved Mental Health**: Resilient individuals are better equipped to handle stress, anxiety, and depression, contributing to overall mental well-being.

3. **Enhanced Problem-Solving Skills**: Resilience encourages a proactive approach to challenges, enabling us to identify practical solutions.

4. **Greater Self-Confidence**: Building resilience boosts self-esteem, empowering us to face challenges positively.

5. **Stronger Relationships**: Resilient individuals maintain healthier relationships by fostering empathy, communication, and mutual support.

Strategies for Building Resilience

Here are strategies for developing resilience and a resilient mindset:

1. **Cultivate a Positive Outlook**: Focus on the positives and maintain optimism. Practice gratitude and celebrate small wins.

2. **Develop Strong Relationships**: Build and sustain supportive connections with friends, family, and colleagues. Offer and seek support from others.

3. **Set Realistic Goals**: Establish achievable goals and break them into manageable steps. Celebrate progress and learn from setbacks.

4. **Practice Self-Care**: Prioritize self-care to support your physical, emotional, and mental well-being through activities like exercise, healthy eating, and relaxation.

5. **Learn from Experiences**: Reflect on past experiences and the lessons they provided. Use these insights to guide future actions and decisions.

6. **Stay Flexible and Open**: Be open to change and adaptable. Embrace new opportunities and view challenges as chances for growth.

7. **Develop Problem-Solving Skills**: Approach challenges with a problem-solving mindset. Break down issues into smaller parts and brainstorm solutions.

8. **Practice Mindfulness**: Engage in mindfulness practices to stay present and aware of your thoughts and emotions, helping you manage stress effectively.

9. **Build Self-Confidence**: Focus on your strengths and achievements, reminding yourself of your capabilities and past successes.

10. **Seek Professional Help**: If necessary, consult therapists, counselors, or coaches for valuable tools and strategies to enhance resilience.

Practical Exercises for Building Resilience

Here are practical exercises to strengthen resilience and develop a resilient mindset:

1. **Gratitude Journaling**: Keep a daily gratitude journal, noting three things you appreciate. Reflect on the positive aspects of your life.

2. **Positive Affirmations**: Create and recite a list of positive affirmations daily that reinforce your resilience and strength.

3. **Problem-Solving Practice**: When faced with challenges, break them down and brainstorm potential solutions, reflecting on past successes.

4. **Mindfulness Meditation**: Dedicate time each day to mindfulness meditation, focusing on your breath and observing thoughts without judgment.

5. **Self-Care Routine**: Establish a self-care routine that prioritizes sleep, nutrition, exercise, and relaxation.

6. **Support System Check-In**: Regularly connect with your support system to share experiences and provide mutual support.

7. **Reflection and Learning**: Reflect on past experiences and the lessons learned to inform future decisions.

8. **Goal Setting**: Write down your goals, break them into actionable steps, and create a timeline to track your progress.

9. **Flexibility Practice**: Foster flexibility by remaining open to new experiences and opportunities.

10. **Professional Support**: Seek assistance from therapists, counselors, or coaches to develop strategies for resilience.

Incorporating these exercises into your daily routine can help you build resilience and develop a mindset that allows you to navigate life's challenges with confidence.

Affirmations

1. I am resilient and capable of overcoming challenges.

2. I am grateful for the lessons that adversity teaches me.

3. I am confident in my ability to adapt to change.

4. I am strong and capable of handling whatever comes my way.

5. I am open to new opportunities and experiences.

6. I am grateful for the support of my loved ones.

7. I am focused on my goals and dreams.

8. I am at peace with myself and my journey.

9. I am confident in my ability to find solutions to problems.

10. I am open to the flow of positive energy and growth.

11. I am grateful for my inner strength and resilience.

12. I am focused on creating a fulfilling and meaningful life.

13. I am confident in my path and direction.

14. I am thankful for the progress I make each day.

15. I am open to learning from my experiences.

16. I am grateful for the support and guidance I receive.

17. I am at peace with the changes in my life.

18. I am focused on my personal growth and development.

19. I am confident in my ability to navigate life's challenges.

20. I am open to new possibilities and opportunities.

21. I am grateful for my journey of personal growth.

Short Meditation

Title: Building Resilience

1. Find a quiet, comfortable place to sit and close your eyes.

2. Take several deep breaths, inhaling through your nose and exhaling through your mouth.

3. Bring your attention to the natural rhythm of your breath.

4. Silently repeat the affirmation: "I am resilient and capable of overcoming challenges."

5. Visualize yourself navigating challenges with confidence and determination, emerging more robust and capable.

6. As you breathe, feel a sense of strength and resilience filling your mind and body.

7. Breathe deeply and repeat the affirmation for a few minutes.

8. When ready, gently open your eyes and return to the present moment.

Chapter 26: Finding Balance in Times of Change

Achieving balance during periods of change is crucial for maintaining well-being and effectively managing transitions. This chapter will discuss the significance of balance, its advantages, and practical strategies for attaining and sustaining equilibrium in your life. We'll explore how balance helps you stay grounded, focused, and resilient.

The Importance of Balance

Balance entails managing various aspects of your life—such as work, relationships, self-care, and personal growth—so that you can flourish. It's about creating harmony, ensuring that no single area overshadows the others. Attaining balance helps you remain centered, particularly during times of change.

Benefits of Finding Balance

Maintaining balance can yield numerous benefits, especially during periods of transition. These benefits include:

1. **Reduced Stress**: Balance helps manage stress by preventing any one area from becoming overwhelming.

2. **Improved Well-Being**: Achieving balance promotes overall physical, emotional, and mental health.

3. **Enhanced Focus**: A balanced life allows for greater concentration on your goals and priorities.

4. **Greater Resilience**: Balance provides stability and support during challenging times, fostering resilience.

5. **Stronger Relationships**: Maintaining balance nurtures healthy relationships by ensuring you have time and energy for loved ones.

Strategies for Finding Balance

Here are some strategies to help you achieve and maintain balance in your life:

1. **Set Priorities**: Identify your key priorities and allocate your time and energy accordingly. Focus on what truly matters.

2. **Create a Schedule**: Develop a daily or weekly schedule that includes time for work, self-care, relationships, and personal growth, ensuring each area is represented.

3. **Practice Mindfulness**: Engage in mindfulness to stay present and aware of your needs and priorities, aiding intentional decision-making.

4. **Set Boundaries**: Establish clear boundaries to protect your time and energy, and communicate them to others to ensure respect.

5. **Engage in Self-Care**: Prioritize self-care activities that support your physical, emotional, and mental well-being, like exercise, healthy eating, and relaxation.

6. **Seek Support**: Connect with friends, family, or support groups for encouragement and guidance, sharing experiences to help maintain balance.

7. **Be Flexible**: Stay open to changes and be willing to adapt. Balance is not static; it requires ongoing evaluation and adjustment.

8. **Reflect and Adjust**: Regularly assess your life to determine if you're maintaining balance, making adjustments as needed to meet your needs.

9. **Practice Gratitude**: Foster an attitude of gratitude by focusing on the positive aspects of your life, which helps ground and center you.

10. **Simplify Your Life**: Streamline your commitments by eliminating unnecessary tasks, and concentrating on what truly matters.

By incorporating these strategies into your daily routine, you can find and maintain balance, staying grounded, focused, and resilient through periods of change.

Affirmations

1. I am committed to finding balance in my life.

2. I am grateful for the harmony and balance I create.

3. I am focused on my top priorities.

4. I am confident in my ability to maintain balance.

5. I am open to adjustments and new experiences.

6. I am grateful for the support of my loved ones.

7. I am at peace with myself and my journey.

8. I am committed to my self-care and well-being.

9. I am confident in my ability to manage stress.

10. I am open to the flow of positive energy and balance.

11. I am grateful for the stability and support I have.

12. I am focused on creating a fulfilling and meaningful life.

13. I am confident in my path and direction.

14. I am thankful for the progress I make each day.

15. I am open to learning from my experiences.

16. I am grateful for the balance and harmony in my life.

17. I am at peace with the changes in my life.

18. I am focused on my personal growth and development.

19. I am confident in my ability to navigate life's challenges.

20. I am open to new possibilities and opportunities.

21. I am grateful for my journey of balance and personal growth.

Short Meditation

Title: Finding Balance

1. Find a quiet, comfortable place to sit and close your eyes.

2. Take several deep breaths, inhaling through your nose and exhaling through your mouth.

3. Bring your attention to the natural rhythm of your breath.

4. Silently repeat the affirmation: "I am committed to finding balance in my life."

5. Visualize yourself creating a balanced and harmonious life with time for work, self-care, relationships, and personal growth.

6. Feel a sense of balance and harmony filling your mind and body as you breathe.

7. Breathe deeply and repeat the affirmation for a few minutes.

8. When ready, gently open your eyes and return to the present moment.

Chapter 27: Cultivating Patience and Persistence

Patience and persistence are vital traits for navigating change and reaching long-term goals. This chapter will delve into their importance, benefits, and practical strategies for fostering these qualities. We'll explore how patience and persistence can help you stay dedicated to your journey and overcome challenges.

The Importance of Patience and Persistence

Patience enables us to remain calm and composed during difficulties, while persistence keeps us committed to our goals despite setbacks. Together, these qualities empower us to face change with resilience and determination, allowing us to continue moving toward our aspirations.

Benefits of Cultivating Patience and Persistence

Developing patience and persistence can lead to numerous advantages, especially when facing change. These benefits include:

1. **Increased Resilience**: Together, patience and persistence enhance our ability to recover from setbacks while staying focused on our objectives.

2. **Improved Problem-Solving Skills**: These traits encourage a solution-oriented approach to challenges, helping us find effective ways to overcome obstacles.

3. **Greater Emotional Stability**: Patience aids in stress management, while persistence fuels motivation and determination.

4. **Enhanced Long-Term Success**: Patience and persistence are essential for achieving long-term goals and maintaining progress.

5. **Stronger Relationships**: These qualities promote empathy, understanding, and effective communication, thereby strengthening our connections with others.

Strategies for Cultivating Patience and Persistence

Here are some practical strategies for integrating patience and persistence into your daily life:

1. **Set Realistic Goals**: Establish achievable goals aligned with your values. Break them down into smaller steps to maintain motivation.

2. **Practice Mindfulness**: Engage in mindfulness practices to remain present and focused, fostering a calm mindset.

3. **Embrace Challenges**: View challenges as opportunities for growth. Approach them positively and with perseverance.

4. **Develop a Growth Mindset**: Cultivate a mindset that values effort and perseverance as keys to success, believing you can improve through dedication.

5. **Reflect on Past Successes**: Recall past instances where you successfully overcame challenges. Use these memories as motivation to stay patient and persistent.

6. **Practice Self-Compassion**: Be kind to yourself, acknowledging your efforts and progress, even if it feels slow.

7. **Create a Support System**: Surround yourself with trusted friends, family, and mentors who can offer encouragement and guidance.

8. **Stay Flexible**: Be willing to adapt your approach. Flexibility is crucial for maintaining persistence and finding solutions.

9. **Use Positive Affirmations**: Repeat affirmations that reinforce your patience and persistence, building self-confidence and motivation.

10. **Celebrate Progress**: Acknowledge and celebrate your achievements, no matter how small, to boost motivation and reinforce persistence.

Practical Exercises for Cultivating Patience and Persistence

Here are some exercises to help integrate patience and persistence into your life:

Embracing Change:

The Spiritual Path to Personal Growth

1. **Goal Setting Exercise**: Write down your goals as actionable steps and create a timeline with milestones to track progress.

2. **Mindfulness Meditation**: Dedicate time each day for mindfulness meditation, focusing on your breath and observing your thoughts.

3. **Positive Affirmations**: Develop a list of affirmations related to patience and persistence, repeating them daily.

4. **Reflection Journal**: Keep a journal to reflect on your experiences, noting challenges, lessons learned, and progress made.

5. **Self-Compassion Practice**: Acknowledge your efforts and progress with kindness, especially during tough times.

6. **Support System Check-In**: Regularly connect with your support system to share experiences and seek encouragement.

7. **Flexibility Practice**: Practice being open to adjustments and new methods, embracing change positively.

8. **Progress Celebration**: Celebrate your achievements to recognize your efforts and inspire continued persistence.

9. **Growth Mindset Reflection**: Reflect on your beliefs about effort and perseverance, fostering a mindset that values improvement through hard work.

10. **Patience Practice**: Focus on the process rather than the outcome, reminding yourself that progress requires time and effort.

Incorporating these exercises into your routine can cultivate patience and persistence, helping you remain committed to your journey and overcome obstacles.

Affirmations

1. I am patient and persistent in achieving my goals.

2. I am grateful for the progress I make each day.

3. I am confident in my ability to overcome challenges.

4. I am open to new opportunities and experiences.

5. I am grateful for the support of my loved ones.

6. I am focused on my goals and dreams.

7. I am at peace with myself and my journey.

8. I am committed to my personal growth and development.

9. I am confident in my ability to find solutions to problems.

10. I am open to the flow of positive energy and growth.

11. I am grateful for my inner strength and resilience.

12. I am focused on creating a fulfilling and meaningful life.

13. I am confident in my path and direction.

14. I am thankful for the progress I make each day.

15. I am open to learning from my experiences.

16. I am grateful for the balance and harmony in my life.

17. I am at peace with the changes in my life.

18. I am focused on my personal growth and development.

19. I am confident in my ability to navigate life's challenges.

20. I am open to new possibilities and opportunities.

21. I am grateful for my journey of personal growth.

Short Meditation

Title: Cultivating Patience and Persistence

1. Find a quiet, comfortable place to sit and close your eyes.

2. Take several deep breaths, inhaling through your nose and exhaling through your mouth.

3. Bring your attention to the natural rhythm of your breath.

4. Silently repeat the affirmation: "I am patient and persistent in achieving my goals."

5. Visualize yourself navigating challenges with patience and persistence, staying committed to your path and achieving your goals.

6. As you breathe, feel a sense of calm and determination filling your mind and body.

7. Breathe deeply and repeat the affirmation for a few minutes.

8. When ready, gently open your eyes and return to the present moment.

Chapter 28: Embracing Change Through Self-Reflection

Self-reflection is a vital tool for personal growth and adapting to change. This chapter examines the significance of self-reflection, its advantages, and actionable strategies to integrate reflective practices into your everyday life. We will explore how self-reflection aids in self-understanding, informed decision-making, and confidently facing change.

The Importance of Self-Reflection

Self-reflection involves analyzing your thoughts, feelings, and behaviors to gain insight into your inner self and experiences. It helps identify your strengths and weaknesses, recognize areas for improvement, and align your actions with your values and goals. Consistent self-reflection keeps you connected to your authentic self, enabling you to navigate change with clarity and purpose.

Benefits of Self-Reflection

Engaging in self-reflection offers numerous advantages, especially during times of change. These include:

1. **Increased Self-Awareness**: It enhances your awareness of your thoughts, emotions, and actions, allowing for more conscious decision-making.

2. **Enhanced Decision-Making**: Reflecting on past experiences provides valuable insights that guide your choices.

3. **Improved Emotional Regulation**: Self-reflection helps you process and manage your emotions, promoting stability and well-being.

4. **Greater Clarity and Purpose**: By reflecting on your values and experiences, you can better define your path and purpose.

5. **Ongoing Personal Growth**: Regular reflection encourages continuous development, helping you adapt and reach your goals.

Strategies for Self-Reflection

To incorporate self-reflection into your daily life, consider these strategies:

1. **Allocate Time for Reflection**: Set aside regular time for self-reflection, whether daily, weekly, or monthly, in a quiet space.

2. **Maintain a Reflection Journal**: Record your thoughts, feelings, and experiences to explore insights about your inner self.

3. **Ask Reflective Questions**: Use guiding questions like "What did I learn today?" or "How can I improve?" to enhance your reflection.

4. **Practice Mindfulness**: Engage in mindfulness to remain present and aware, enriching your self-reflection with a non-judgmental perspective.

5. **Reflect on Past Experiences**: Analyze past events to identify patterns and lessons that contribute to your growth.

6. **Set Goals and Intentions**: Use self-reflection to establish clear personal growth goals and adjust them as needed.

7. **Seek Feedback**: Ask for insights from trusted friends, family, or mentors to deepen your self-reflection.

8. **Practice Self-Compassion**: Approach self-reflection gently, recognizing your efforts and being kind to yourself as you explore areas for growth.

9. **Utilize Reflective Tools**: Use guided journals or reflective exercises to support your practice.

10. **Reflect on Your Values**: Regularly assess your core values and how they align with your current path.

Practical Exercises for Self-Reflection

Here are practical exercises to help incorporate self-reflection into your life:

1. **Daily Reflection Journal**: Keep a journal to write down your daily thoughts and feelings, identifying insights and patterns.

2. **Reflective Questions**: Use questions to guide your reflection, writing down your answers to explore deeper insights.

3. **Mindfulness Meditation**: Dedicate time each day to meditate, focusing on your breath and observing your thoughts non-judgmentally.

4. **Past Experience Reflection**: Reflect on past experiences to extract lessons and understand their impact on your beliefs and actions.

5. **Goal Setting and Reflection**: Set personal growth goals and periodically reflect on your progress.

6. **Feedback Reflection**: Consider insights from trusted individuals to enhance your self-reflection process.

7. **Self-Compassion Practice**: Acknowledge your progress with kindness, especially when exploring challenging areas.

8. **Guided Journals**: Use journals with prompts to facilitate your reflective practice.

9. **Values Reflection**: Regularly check if your actions align with your core values.

10. **Reflection Rituals**: Establish regular rituals for self-reflection, like weekly reviews.

Incorporating these exercises into your daily routine can strengthen your self-reflection practice, helping you understand yourself better, make informed decisions, and embrace change with confidence.

Affirmations

1. I am committed to self-reflection and personal growth.

2. I am grateful for the insights and clarity I gained.

3. I am open to exploring my thoughts and feelings.

4. I am confident in my ability to understand myself better.

5. I am at peace with my journey of self-discovery.

6. I am open to the lessons and experiences that shape me.

7. I am grateful for my inner wisdom and guidance.

8. I am focused on my personal growth and development.

9. I am confident in my ability to navigate change.

10. I am open to the flow of positive energy and growth.

11. I am grateful for the support of my loved ones.

12. I am committed to aligning my actions with my values.

13. I am at peace with my past experiences.

14. I am open to new insights and understanding.

15. I am grateful for the clarity and purpose in my life.

16. I am confident in my path and direction.

17. I am focused on creating a fulfilling and meaningful life.

18. I am open to the flow of positive energy and growth.

19. I am grateful for the progress I make each day.

20. I am committed to my journey of self-reflection and growth.

21. I am at peace with the changes in my life.

Short Meditation

Title: Embracing Self-Reflection

1. Find a quiet, comfortable place to sit and close your eyes.

2. Take several deep breaths, inhaling through your nose and exhaling through your mouth.

3. Bring your attention to the natural rhythm of your breath.

4. Silently repeat the affirmation: "I am committed to self-reflection and personal growth."

5. Visualize yourself exploring your thoughts, feelings, and experiences with an open and curious mind.

6. As you breathe, feel a sense of clarity and understanding filling your mind and body.

7. Breathe deeply and repeat the affirmation for a few minutes.

8. When ready, gently open your eyes and return to the present moment.

Chapter 29: The Power of Gratitude

Gratitude is a powerful practice that can transform your perspective and improve your overall well-being. In this chapter, we will look at the concept of gratitude, its benefits, and practical strategies for incorporating it into your daily life. We will talk about how gratitude can help you navigate change, foster resilience, and cultivate a positive mindset.

The Concept of Gratitude

Gratitude entails acknowledging and appreciating the positive aspects of your life. It is about acknowledging the big and small gifts you receive each day and expressing thanks for them. Practicing gratitude shifts your focus from what you lack to what you have, cultivating a sense of abundance and fulfillment.

Benefits of Practicing Gratitude

Incorporating gratitude into daily life can bring numerous benefits, especially when navigating change. These benefits include:

1. **Enhanced Well-Being**: Gratitude enhances well-being by fostering positive emotions and reducing stress and anxiety.

2. **Increased Resilience**: Practicing gratitude helps you stay positive and resilient in facing challenges and setbacks.

3. **Improved Relationships**: Expressing gratitude strengthens your relationships by fostering empathy, appreciation, and connection.

4. **Greater Happiness**: Gratitude increases happiness and satisfaction, enhancing the overall quality of life.

5. **Heightened Self-Awareness**: Gratitude promotes self-reflection and awareness, helping you appreciate your strengths and achievements.

Strategies for Practicing Gratitude

Here are some strategies for incorporating gratitude into your daily life and reaping its benefits:

1. Keep a Gratitude Journal: List three things you are grateful for daily. Reflect on these positive aspects and how they improve your life.

2. Express Thanks to Others: Take the time to appreciate the people who support and inspire you. Expressing gratitude strengthens your relationships and fosters a sense of connection.

3. Practice Mindful Gratitude: Focus on what you are grateful for during your mindfulness practice. Allow yourself to experience the feelings of appreciation and joy fully.

4. Use Gratitude Affirmations: Repeat gratitude affirmations to reinforce a positive mindset. Examples include "I am grateful for the abundance in my life" and "I appreciate the support of my loved ones."

5. Reflect on Positive Experiences: Reflect on positive experiences and what you learned. Acknowledge the growth and insights acquired from these experiences.

6. Create a Gratitude Jar: List the things you are grateful for on small pieces of paper and place them in a jar. Review them regularly to remind yourself of the positive aspects of your life.

7. Practice Gratitude in Challenging Times: During difficult times, think of what you are grateful for. This practice can help you stay positive and resilient.

8. Share Your Gratitude: Express your gratitude with others through conversations, social media, or other forms of communication. Sharing gratitude spreads positivity and inspiration.

9. Incorporate Gratitude into Your Routine: Make gratitude a part of your daily routine, such as during meals, before bed, or upon waking. Consistency helps reinforce the habit.

10. Meditate on Gratitude: Use meditation to focus on gratitude. Visualize the things you are grateful for and allow yourself to feel the associated positive emotions.

Practical Exercises for Practicing Gratitude

Here are some practical exercises to help you incorporate gratitude into your daily life:

1. Daily Gratitude Journal: Keep a daily journal to write down three things you are thankful for each day. Reflect on these positive aspects and how they enhance your life.

2. Thank You Notes: Write thank you notes to people who have positively impacted your life. Express your appreciation and gratitude for their support and kindness.

3. Mindful Gratitude Practice: Schedule time daily to focus on what you are grateful for. Allow yourself to experience the feelings of appreciation and joy fully.

4. Gratitude Affirmations: Create a list of gratitude affirmations and repeat them daily. Use affirmations that resonate with you and reinforce a positive mindset.

5. Gratitude Reflection: Think of your positive experiences and what you learned. Acknowledge the growth and insights gained from these experiences.

6. Gratitude Jar: List the things you are grateful for on small pieces of paper and place them in a jar. Review them regularly to remind yourself of the positive aspects of your life.

7. Gratitude in Challenging Times: During difficult times, think of what you are grateful for. This practice can help you stay positive and resilient.

8. Share Your Gratitude: Share your gratitude with others through conversations, social media, or other forms of communication. Sharing gratitude spreads positivity and inspiration.

9. Gratitude Routine: Include gratitude in your daily routine, such as during meals, before bed, or upon waking. Consistency helps reinforce the habit.

10. Gratitude Meditation: Use meditation to focus on gratitude. Visualize the things you are grateful for and allow yourself to feel the associated positive emotions.

By incorporating these exercises into your daily routine, you can cultivate gratitude, which will help you navigate change, foster resilience, and develop a positive mindset.

Affirmations

1. I am grateful for the abundance in my life.

2. I am thankful for the support of my loved ones.

3. I am open to receiving and appreciating the positive aspects of my life.

4. I am grateful for the lessons and growth from my experiences.

5. I am thankful for the opportunities that come my way.

6. I am open to the flow of positive energy and gratitude.

7. I am grateful for my inner strength and resilience.

8. I am thankful for the beauty and wonder of the world around me.

9. I am open to new experiences and opportunities for growth.

10. I am grateful for my journey of personal growth.

11. I am thankful for the progress I make each day.

12. I am open to the support and encouragement of others.

13. I am grateful for the love and connection in my life.

14. I am thankful for the clarity and purpose in my life.

15. I am open to the flow of positive energy and growth.

16. I am grateful for the balance and harmony in my life.

17. I am thankful for the lessons and experiences that have shaped me.

18. I am open to the flow of abundance and gratitude.

19. I am grateful for the progress I make each day.

20. I am thankful for the support and guidance I receive.

21. I am open to the flow of positive energy and gratitude in my life.

Short Meditation

Title: Embracing Gratitude

1. Find a quiet, comfortable place to sit and close your eyes.

2. Take several deep breaths, inhaling through your nose and exhaling through your mouth.

3. Bring your attention to the natural rhythm of your breath.

4. Silently repeat the affirmation: "I am grateful for the abundance in my life."

5. Visualize what you are grateful for and allow yourself to feel the associated positive emotions.

6. As you breathe, feel a sense of gratitude and appreciation filling your mind and body.

7. Breathe deeply and repeat the affirmation for a few minutes.

8. When ready, gently open your eyes and return to the present moment.

Chapter 30: Embracing Change as an Ongoing Journey

Change is a constant element of life. By viewing change as an ongoing journey, we can navigate transitions with resilience and purpose. This chapter emphasizes the importance of perceiving change as a continuous process, outlines its benefits, and offers practical strategies for embracing change throughout life. We will focus on developing a mindset that welcomes growth and commitment to personal evolution.

The Continuous Nature of Change

Change is not merely a singular event but a continual process that influences our lives. Acknowledging this ongoing nature allows us to be more adaptable and receptive to new experiences. By embracing change as a journey, we can view each transition as a chance for personal growth and self-improvement.

Advantages of Viewing Change as an Ongoing Journey

Seeing change as a continuous journey can yield various benefits, including:

1. **Enhanced Adaptability**: Recognizing the constant nature of change helps us adjust quickly to new situations.

2. **Improved Resilience**: Accepting that change is inevitable fosters resilience, enabling us to recover from challenges more effectively.

3. **Ongoing Personal Growth**: Continuous change provides numerous opportunities for learning and development.

4. **Greater Self-Awareness**: Embracing change encourages regular self-reflection, leading to deeper self-understanding.

5. **Sustained Motivation**: Viewing change as a journey helps maintain a commitment to personal growth.

Strategies for Embracing Change as an Ongoing Journey

To integrate this mindset into your daily life, consider the following strategies:

1. **Cultivate a Growth Mindset**: Adopt a perspective that views change as a chance for learning and improvement.

2. **Practice Self-Reflection**: Regularly evaluate your thoughts and experiences to gain insights into your growth.

3. **Set Long-Term Goals**: Establish goals that align with your values and break them into manageable steps.

4. **Stay Open to New Experiences**: Embrace new opportunities with curiosity and a willingness to learn.

5. **Develop Resilience**: Build strong support networks and practice self-care to maintain a positive outlook.

6. **Celebrate Progress**: Acknowledge even small achievements to reinforce your commitment to growth.

7. **Remain Flexible**: Be willing to adjust your plans as necessary to navigate change effectively.

8. **Engage in Lifelong Learning**: Commit to acquiring new knowledge and skills that enhance your personal growth.

9. **Embrace Uncertainty**: Accept uncertainty as a natural part of life and trust in your ability to adapt.

10. **Practice Gratitude**: Regularly recognize and appreciate the positive aspects of your life, fostering a grounded mindset.

Practical Exercises for Embracing Change as an Ongoing Journey

Incorporate these exercises into your routine to embrace change more fully:

1. **Growth Mindset Journal**: Document your experiences and the lessons learned from adapting to change.

2. **Long-Term Goal Setting**: Write down and break down your long-term goals into actionable steps.

3. **New Experience Challenge**: Try something new regularly and reflect on the insights gained.

4. **Resilience Building**: Engage in activities that foster resilience, such as mindfulness and exercise.

5. **Progress Celebration**: Regularly recognize and celebrate your achievements to motivate yourself.

6. **Flexibility Practice**: Remain open to new methods and changes in your plans.

7. **Lifelong Learning Plan**: Outline your areas of interest and set goals for acquiring new skills.

8. **Embrace Uncertainty Meditation**: Meditate on the concept of uncertainty and visualize navigating it confidently.

9. **Gratitude Practice**: Keep a gratitude journal to highlight positive aspects of your life daily.

10. **Reflection Rituals**: Establish regular self-reflection sessions to explore your thoughts and feelings.

By adopting these practices, you can embrace change as a continuous journey, allowing you to navigate life's transitions with resilience and purpose.

Affirmations

1. I am embracing change as a continuous journey.

2. I am open to new experiences and opportunities for growth.

3. I am confident in my ability to adapt and thrive.

4. I am grateful for the lessons and growth from my experiences.

5. I am committed to my personal growth and development.

6. I am open to the flow of positive energy and transformation.

7. I am grateful for my inner strength and resilience.

8. I am focused on creating a fulfilling and meaningful life.

9. I am confident in my path and direction.

10. I am thankful for the progress I make each day.

11. I am open to learning from my experiences.

12. I am grateful for the support and guidance I receive.

13. I am at peace with the changes in my life.

14. I am focused on my personal growth and development.

15. I am confident in my ability to navigate life's challenges.

16. I am open to new possibilities and opportunities.

17. I am grateful for my journey of personal growth.

18. I am committed to embracing change with grace and resilience.

19. I am open to the flow of positive energy and growth.

20. I am thankful for the balance and harmony in my life.

21. I am at peace with the continuous journey of change.

Short Meditation

Title: Embracing Change as a Continuous Journey

1. Find a quiet, comfortable place to sit and close your eyes.

2. Take several deep breaths, inhaling through your nose and exhaling through your mouth.

3. Bring your attention to the natural rhythm of your breath.

4. Silently repeat the affirmation: "I am embracing change as a continuous journey."

5. Visualize yourself navigating life's changes with grace, resilience, and purpose.

6. As you breathe, feel a sense of peace and confidence filling your mind and body.

7. Breathe deeply and repeat the affirmation for a few minutes.

8. When ready, gently open your eyes and return to the present moment.

Conclusion: Embracing the Journey of Change

As we conclude this exploration, it's essential to recognize that change is a continuous journey that affects every aspect of our lives. We have examined various methods for embracing change, cultivating resilience, and fostering growth. Let's distill these lessons into an inspiring conclusion.

Embracing Change: A Continuous Journey

Change is a constant truth that influences our lives. Through change, we grow, learn, and discover our true selves. By embracing it as a journey, we open ourselves to endless possibilities. Though this path is often filled with challenges, it is within these moments that we find our strength and purpose.

The Power of Self-Reflection and Growth

Self-reflection has illuminated our path toward greater self-awareness. By regularly evaluating our experiences, we align our actions with our values, promoting continuous growth. Remember, this practice focuses on progress, not perfection.

Cultivating Patience and Persistence

Patience and persistence are crucial in navigating change. They remind us that growth takes time, and setbacks are part of the journey. By nurturing these qualities, we strengthen our resolve to overcome obstacles.

The Transformative Power of Gratitude

Gratitude shifts our focus from lack to abundance, enhancing our well-being. By integrating gratitude into our lives, we foster a positive mindset that supports our journey through change.

Embracing Creativity and Intuition

Creativity and intuition guide us in navigating change, helping us explore new perspectives and make decisions aligned with our true selves. Embracing these qualities opens us to new possibilities.

The Strength of Resilience and Balance

Resilience allows us to recover from setbacks, while balance helps us manage different life aspects, ensuring no single area overwhelms us. Together, they create a stable foundation for our journey.

The Role of Spirituality and Connection

Spirituality provides deeper meaning and connection. It reminds us that our journey is sacred and transformative. Nurturing this connection gives us strength and inspiration as we embrace change.

A Journey of Infinite Possibilities

Remember that embracing change is a lifelong journey filled with endless possibilities. Each chapter of life offers new growth opportunities. Approach this journey with curiosity and courage, trusting in your ability to navigate change and create a fulfilling life that reflects your true self.

Celebrate your progress, honor your experiences, and remain committed to your personal growth. Embrace change with wonder and gratitude, knowing that each step brings you closer to your best self. Your journey is a beautiful, ever-evolving masterpiece.

Final Affirmations

1. I am embracing the journey of change with an open heart and mind.

2. I am grateful for the infinite possibilities that change brings.

3. I am confident in navigating life's transitions gracefully and resiliently.

4. I am open to continuous growth and self-improvement.

5. I am thankful for the lessons and experiences that have shaped me.

6. I am committed to my journey of personal and spiritual growth.

7. I am embracing my true self and highest potential.

With this conclusion, may you begin your journey of change with renewed inspiration, strength, and a deep sense of purpose. The path ahead is yours to shape, filled with limitless opportunities and boundless growth. Embrace it fully and let your journey of change be a testament to your courage, resilience, and unwavering spirit.

Acknowledgments

As I begin this journey of sharing my spiritual path through this book, I am overwhelmed with appreciation for the many people who have influenced my life and contributed to my growth. This work is more than just a reflection of my experiences; it is a tapestry made from the love, wisdom, and support of countless souls who have journeyed alongside me.

First and foremost, my heartfelt thanks go to the **Church of Christ **. Since I was a young adolescent of 13, this community has been my spiritual anchor, nurturing my understanding of God and guiding me through life's myriad challenges. The teachings and fellowship I have received there have been instrumental in shaping my spiritual foundation. For over 30 years, you have entrusted me with the sacred responsibility of being your spiritual guide; I am eternally grateful. Your unwavering faith and support have been a light in my life.

I sincerely appreciate my high school teachers, who imparted invaluable lessons about making wise choices. You taught me the significance of steering clear of life's temptations and instilled a reverent fear of God, reminding me that his watchful eyes guide us to righteousness. Your teachings were not just academic; they were life lessons that have stayed with me, helping me navigate the world's complexities with integrity and faith.

Words fail to capture the depth of my gratitude to my beloved wife, **Magy**. Your unconditional love and unwavering support have been the bedrock of my existence. You have supported me in every endeavor, offering encouragement and strength. Your belief in me fuels my spirit, and your love is the sanctuary to which I always return. Thank you for being my partner in life and faith.

To my son, **Pierre Arthur**, who cherishes me and proudly calls me his father, your love and respect deeply move me. Your pride in my identity reflects our bond, and I am honored to be your father. You inspire me to be the best version of myself, and I am grateful for the joy and fulfillment you bring into my life.

To my daughter-in-law, **Jamie Carneiro**, I extend a heartfelt thank you for the love and respect you have shown me. Since you became part of our family, your kindness and warmth have been a source of joy and comfort. You have embraced our family openly, and your love for my son has strengthened our bonds. Thank you for being a shining example of love and compassion and enriching our lives with your presence.

To my daughter, **Melissah**, your respectful love and gentle spirit are treasures I hold dear. Your presence in my life constantly reminds me of the beauty and grace that love can bring. Thank you for your kindness and for enriching my life with warmth and compassion.

To my beloved daughter, **Christelle**: Your insight and empathy touch my heart deeply. You genuinely grasp the infinite love I have for you. Your wisdom is remarkable for your age, and your understanding of my journey fills me with immense pride. Thank you for being a constant source of strength and inspiration.

Reflecting on the journey that has brought me to this moment, I am reminded of the incredible family who has stood by me with love and acceptance. I sincerely thank my sister-in-law, **Linda C. Pierre**. For the past 37 years, Linda, you have embraced me with a love that is unwavering and true. Your acceptance and kindness have been a source of comfort, and I am profoundly grateful for our bond. You have always supported me, celebrating my victories and offering sage advice during challenges. Your presence in my life is a blessing, and I am thankful for your love and friendship.

To my mother-in-law, **Heureuse Cadet**, your unconditional love and acceptance have been a gift beyond measure. From the moment I entered your family as a young teenager, uncertain and still learning the true meaning of love, you welcomed me with open arms. You have treated me as your son, offering guidance, support, and a love that has remained constant through the years. Your faith in me has been a source of strength, and I am eternally grateful for the warmth and kindness you have shown me. Thank you for being a pillar of love and enriching my life with your nurturing spirit.

To my beloved sister-in-law, **Yanick C. Charles**, who has passed away but remains ever-present in my heart, I owe a debt of gratitude that words can scarcely contain. Yanick, you always believed in me and trusted me with every decision I made. In times when life presented challenges and uncertainties, you were my refuge—my confidante and friend. Your unwavering faith in me has been a guiding light, encouraging me to pursue my dreams and stay true to myself. Though you are no longer with us in body, I feel your spirit alongside me, offering support and love as I continue my journey. Your memory is a cherished part of my life, and your legacy of kindness and trust lives on in the hearts of all who knew you.

I sincerely thank my sister-in-law, Edwyigh Franck, for your invaluable lessons. Your wisdom and insights have shaped my understanding and approach to life. I love you unconditionally, and through your lessons, I found inspiration to write this book. Your guidance has encouraged me to reflect deeply and share my journey with others; I am profoundly thankful.

In acknowledging these remarkable women, I am reminded of the profound impact of love, support, and acceptance on one's life. Each of you has contributed to my journey in unique and significant ways, and I am deeply grateful for the roles you have played in my life. Through your love and encouragement, I have found the strength to pursue my passions and share my story with the world.

As I continue to walk the path of life, I carry with me the lessons and love you have imparted. Thank you for being a part of my journey, believing in me, and showing me the true meaning of family. Your love is a gift that I treasure, and I am honored to have you in my life.

I am profoundly grateful to the **Sunrise Spiritual Family**, who have embraced my newfound spirituality and embarked on this journey with me. Your open heart and willingness to explore new spiritual horizons have been a source of encouragement and hope. Together, we have forged a path of discovery and growth, and I am honored to walk this journey with you.

I also wish to acknowledge those I had the privilege to teach before their passing. Your presence in my life was a gift, and your forgiveness for any past spiritual ignorance is a testament to your grace and understanding. I believe that your spirits continue to guide me on this journey, and I am thankful for the lessons you have taught.

To my dear friend Renezil Jean Claude, who has been a steadfast companion for over 50 years, your friendship is a blessing beyond measure. Even when the world turned against me for my new understanding of spirituality, you remained by my side, unwavering in your loyalty. Our relationship transcends doctrinal differences, rooted in a deep and abiding love I cherish dearly. Thank you for your steadfast support and for being a true friend in every sense of the word.

Finally, I extend my gratitude to my publishers and editors, whose expertise and dedication have been instrumental in bringing this book to life. Your guidance and insight have helped shape my words into a narrative that I hope will resonate with readers on their spiritual journeys. Thank you for your commitment to this project and for believing in its message.

In closing, I am reminded that this book is a product of my efforts, and a collective endeavor made possible by so much love, support, and guidance. To every one of you, I offer my deepest thanks. May this work serve as a testament to the power of community, the strength of love, and the profound impact each of us can have on one another's spiritual journey.

About the Author

In the vast tapestry of human experience, few journeys are as profound and transformative as the spiritual path. My name is **Pierre Etienne**, and I have dedicated over three decades to serving as a church minister for the Church of Christ. I have conducted hundreds of baptisms, officiated countless weddings, and provided solace during funerals. My journey has been deep reflection, questioning, and, ultimately, embracing change. This Journey seeks to illuminate my spiritual evolution, the lessons learned, and the insights shared in this book, **Embracing Change: The Spiritual Path to Personal Growth**.

Early Encounters with the Divine

From a tender age, I was blessed—or perhaps burdened—with experiences that would shape my understanding of spirituality. Between the ages of four and ten, I frequently encountered what I believed to be guardian angels. In my youthful imagination, these ethereal beings were majestic figures with wings, reminiscent of the biblical accounts of divine messengers. However, when I shared these experiences with my parents, I was met with skepticism. They dismissed my encounters as mere illusions or dreams, leaving me in a state of confusion.

This early dismissal of my spiritual experiences planted seeds of doubt within me. I began to question the nature of reality and the existence of the divine. As I grew older, I found solace in the teachings of the Church, where I dedicated my life to guiding others toward salvation. Yet, the echoes of my childhood experiences lingered, urging me to seek a deeper understanding of spirituality beyond the confines of doctrine.

The Dichotomy of Theory and Practice

As a minister, I was steeped in theological teachings emphasizing the importance of faith, baptism, and the promise of eternal life. I preached about Adam's fall and the necessity of accepting Jesus Christ to attain forgiveness and a relationship with God. However, beneath my sermons lay a persistent questioning of the truths I espoused. I often found myself in deep contemplation, pondering the validity of my teachings and the evidence that supported them.

Every sermon I delivered was not merely a performance; it was a dialogue with my soul. I would walk the streets, visit parks, or even take showers, engaging in conversations with the universe. I asked myself profound questions: **Is it true? What evidence do I have to certify that what I say is true? ** These inquiries became the foundation of my spiritual journey, propelling me toward a quest for authenticity.

The Turning Point

In late 2015, a pivotal moment occurred that would forever alter the trajectory of my spiritual path. While watching the film The Secret by Rhonda Byrne, I heard an inner voice urging me to pay close attention. This voice was unlike anything I had experienced; it resonated with a truth that transcended my previous understanding. As I watched the film repeatedly, the veil of ignorance began to lift, revealing a world of possibilities I had never considered.

This awakening prompted me to explore various spiritual practices and invest in many spiritual books. The results were astonishing. I began to experience a profound shift in my consciousness, leading me to discard the theological texts that had once guided my teachings. I realized that my previous beliefs about salvation and damnation were rooted in fear rather than love.

A New Understanding of Spirituality

As I delved deeper into my spiritual exploration, I understood that spirituality is not confined to any doctrine or belief system. It is a vast, ever-evolving journey that invites us to embrace change and growth. I came to see that the divine is not limited to the pages of scripture but is present in every moment, every interaction, and every experience.

This realization was both liberating and daunting. I had spent years teaching that those who did not adhere to my beliefs were destined for eternal damnation. This knowledge was heavy on my heart, and I felt compelled to seek forgiveness from those I had misled. In a moment of vulnerability, I stood before my congregation and confessed that I had been living a lie. I asked for their forgiveness, acknowledging the pain my teachings may have caused.

The Response to Change

The reaction to my confession was mixed. Some congregation members believed I was joking, while others thought I had lost my mind. Yet, a significant portion of my community began to resonate with my newfound understanding. They expressed gratitude for my honesty and joined me on this journey of spiritual exploration. Together, we began to practice new forms of spirituality, embracing the idea that we are all interconnected, and that love is the ultimate guiding force.

However, not everyone was supportive. Some long-time friends distanced themselves from me, and confident religious leaders labeled me as an agent of Satan. They accused me of leading souls astray, yet I remained steadfast in my commitment to truth. I understood that the path of authenticity often comes with challenges, but I was willing to face them for spiritual growth.

The Power of Spiritual Practice

In the years following my spiritual awakening, I dedicated myself to practicing spirituality with my newfound knowledge. Alongside the members of my congregation who chose to stay with me, we embarked on a journey of exploration and growth. We delved into various spiritual practices, embracing meditation, reflection, and open dialogue as tools for self-discovery. Since the onset of the COVID-19 pandemic, our gatherings have transitioned to a virtual format, allowing us to continue our journey every Sunday via Zoom **(Zoom Meeting**

https://us02web.zoom.us/j/3262604671?pwd=TW9vRm1Y NjdiQW53cWxEWkFabTRDUT09

Meeting ID: 326 260 4671

Passcode: SSF66WAY). This adaptation has enabled us to maintain our sense of community and connection, even during physical separation.

The practice was simple yet profound. We engaged in meditation, reflection, and open dialogue, allowing the group's energy to guide us. Participants began to share their experiences of transformation, and together, we cultivated a community rooted in love and acceptance. The results were remarkable; individuals reported feeling more connected to themselves, each other, and the divine.

The Journey of Writing

As I continued to explore my spiritual path, I felt compelled to share my experiences and insights with a broader audience. This led to the creation of this book, **Embracing Change: The Spiritual Path to Personal Growth**. In this work, I delve into the lessons learned throughout my journey, offering readers a roadmap for their spiritual exploration.

The book is not merely a collection of teachings; it is an invitation to embark on a journey of self-discovery. I encourage readers to question their beliefs, embrace their experiences, and seek the truth within themselves. Through personal anecdotes, spiritual practices, and reflections, I aim to inspire others to embrace change as a catalyst for growth.

The Essence of Spirituality

The core of my teachings is the understanding that spirituality is a deeply personal journey. It is not confined to the walls of a church or the pages of a book; it is woven into the fabric of our everyday lives. Each moment presents an opportunity for growth, healing, and connection. I believe the divine is present in the mundane, waiting for us to awaken to its presence.

As I reflect on my journey, I am reminded of the words of Sigmund Freud: **"The interpretation of dreams is the royal road to a knowledge of the unconscious activities of the mind."** This quote resonates deeply with me, as I have learned that our literal and metaphorical dreams hold profound significance. They are windows into our souls, revealing the desires, fears, and truths beneath the surface.

Embracing Change as a Spiritual Practice

Embracing change is not merely a concept; it is a spiritual practice that invites us to let go of the familiar and step into the unknown. It requires courage, vulnerability, and a willingness to confront our fears. Change can be uncomfortable, but it is often through discomfort that we experience the most profound growth.

This book explores various practices that can help individuals navigate changing challenges. These include mindfulness, meditation, affirmations, journaling, and community engagement. Each practice serves as a tool for self-reflection and connection, allowing us to cultivate a deeper understanding of ourselves and our place in the world.

The Role of Community

Throughout my journey, I have come to appreciate the importance of community in the spiritual path. We are not meant to walk this journey alone; we are called to support one another, share our experiences, and learn from each other. The connections we forge with others can serve as mirrors, reflecting our growth and challenges.

In my spiritual gatherings, I have witnessed the power of community firsthand. Individuals from diverse backgrounds come together, united by a shared desire for growth and understanding. In this space, we celebrate our differences and honor our unique journeys. We create a tapestry of love, acceptance, and spiritual exploration.

Conclusion

Reflecting on my journey as a church minister and spiritual seeker, I am grateful for the lessons learned and shared experiences. This book, **Embracing Change: The Spiritual Path to Personal Growth**, is a testament to the transformative power of spirituality. It invites all who seek to deepen their understanding of themselves and their connection to the divine.

In a chaotic and uncertain world, embracing change is a beacon of hope. It reminds us that our past does not define us but are continually evolving beings capable of growth and transformation. I invite you to join me on this journey, question, explore, and embrace the beauty of change. Together, we can navigate the spiritual path toward personal growth, discovering the truth within us all.

Join Our Weekly Spiritual Journey: Live Reflections and Meditations

Dear Reader,

Thank you for choosing "Embracing Change: The Spiritual Path to Personal Growth." We warmly invite you to join us for weekly reflections and meditations that will profoundly transform your spiritual and personal life.

**When: ** Every Sunday, 8:30 am to 9:30 am

**Where: ** Zoom Meeting

[Join Here] (https://us02web.zoom.us/j/3262604671?pwd=TW9vRm1YNjd iQW53cWxEWkFabTRDUT09)

**Meeting ID: ** 326 260 4671

**Passcode: ** SSF66WAY

We look forward to sharing this transformative journey with you.

With gratitude,

Pierre Etienne,

Metaphysician and spiritual counselor

www.ingramcontent.com/pod-product-compliance
Lightning Source LLC
Chambersburg PA
CBHW021137130626
46554CB00005B/1545